Thou Remainest

A selection of papers setting forth the excellency and sufficiency of the Lord Jesus Christ

J. Wilson Smith

Scripture Truth Publications

THOU REMAINEST

All but two of the chapters in this book were first published as articles in "Scripture Truth" magazine between 1909 and 1919.

First published 1920 by The Central Bible Truth Depôt, 5, Rose Street, Paternoster Square, London, E.C.4.

Reprinted c.1930 by The Central Bible Truth Depôt, 5, Rose Street, Paternoster Square, London, E.C.4.

Re-typeset and transferred to digital printing 2013

ISBN: 978-0-901860-04-0 (paperback)

Copyright © 1909-19 The Central Bible Truth Depôt and 2013 Scripture Truth Publications in this edition

A publication of Scripture Truth

All rights reserved. No part of this publication may be reproduced, stored in a retrieval system, or transmitted, in any form or by any means, electronic, mechanical, photocopying, recording or otherwise without prior permission of Scripture Truth Publications.

Most quotations are taken from The Authorized (King James) Version. Rights in the Authorized Version are vested in the Crown. Reproduced by permission of the Crown's patentee, Cambridge University Press.

Some alternative readings quote from "The Holy Scriptures, a New Translation from the Original Languages" by J. N. Darby (G Morrish, 1890)

References to the Revised Version are to "The New Testament of our Lord and Saviour Jesus Christ, Translated out of the Greek: Being the Version Set Forth A.D. 1611, Compared with the Most Ancient Authorities and Revised, A.D. 1881". Oxford: Oxford University Press, 1881 or "The Holy Bible containing the Old and New Testaments translated out of the original tongues : being the version set forth A.D. 1611 compared with the most ancient authorities and revised". Oxford: University Press, 1885.

Cover photograph © Mr Doomits - Fotolia.com

Published by Scripture Truth Publications
31-33 Glover Street, Crewe, Cheshire, CW1 3LD

Scripture Truth is an imprint of Central Bible Hammond Trust, a charitable trust

Typesetting by John Rice
Printed and bound by Lightning Source

FOREWORD

The following papers, with two exceptions, have appeared at intervals in "Scripture Truth"; consequently, my eye was always one of the first to scan them. They were all received with thankfulness and read with profit and refreshment, not because the writer of them is one of the best of friends, and most faithful of yoke-fellows in the Lord's service that I know; nor because he writes with a clearness and charm which few can command—both are true—but because his theme is always Christ.

For more than half a century he has proved and sung the truth of those precious words:—

> "O Christ, He is the fountain,
> The deep sweet well of love;
> The streams on earth I've tasted,
> More deep I'll drink above."

Hence he writes, not worn-out platitudes, nor of untried theories, but of a Person, well-known, out of the fullness of a heart that finds its joy in the Lord.

He discovered in early life as a young army officer with great ambitions, that our Lord Jesus Christ was enough for his soul's salvation; a brighter and better portion than the brightest and best that the world could offer; and all through life's joys and sorrows he has found Him to be enough—the never-changing, ever gracious, infinitely tender Saviour, Master, Lord and Friend.

It has been his joy through the changing years to serve the Lord in the Gospel, and to see many, very many, gladly follow the One whom he preached; and now in old age, having stood beside the open graves of most of the dearly-loved fellow-labourers for Christ of his vigorous days, and of one nearer and dearer than all, unable as formerly to tramp the open roads telling out the glad Evangel, he still rejoices in the excellency of the knowledge of Christ Jesus his Lord, and would turn our thoughts to Him Who "dieth no more"; and, with this end in view, he gives us this little volume with its appropriate title,

"THOU REMAINEST."

May God, even the Father, richly bless it.

Yes, the servants of the Lord come and go; the ruthless hand of time changes everything beneath the sun; the world itself grows old, but Christ abides; and He is sufficient for all the vast needs of His saints on earth until He comes again; and then shall He still abide, the all-satisfying and eternally glorious object of the heart of His church—the Lamb's wife.

And this I know well is the present joy and certain hope of the author.

J. T. Mawson

CONTENTS

Foreword 3
Everlasting glory (poem) 6
The All-sufficient One 7
God's Present Ministry 11
Christ the Creator 15
"A Saviour, Jesus" 18
The Angels and the Magi 22
"Never Man Spake Like This Man" 27
"Jesus Wept" 31
The Son of God 35
A Word to the Weary 40
"Jesus the Son of God" 44
Christ our Pattern 49
The Cross of Christ 54
The Risen Lord 57
Christ's Priesthood 61
"The Coming of the Lord Draweth Nigh" 65
The Bridegroom 69
The Coming King 74
King of Kings (poem) 78
"My Glory" 79
Praise 83
Bridal Affection and Brotherly Love 87
"For the Sake of the Name" 92
The Last Psalm 96
Love's Retreat (poem) 99

EVERLASTING glory be,
God and Father, unto Thee!
'Tis with joy Thy children raise
Hearts and voices in Thy praise.

Thine the light that showed our sin,
Showed how guilty we had been:
Thine the love that us to save
Thine own Son for sinners gave.

Called to share the rest of God
In the Father's blest abode,
God of love and God of light
In Thy praises we unite.

Gladly we Thy grace proclaim,
Knowing now the Father's Name:
God and Father, unto Thee
Everlasting glory be!

The All-sufficient One

"Thou remainest"—Psalm 102:26, and Hebrews 1:11.

TWO wonderful words indeed, and worthy of the deepest appreciation. They refer to One who is placed in connection with creation in its widest extent, the heavens and the earth, but which, while transitory and perishable, leaves Him unaffected by their removal. He "continues still", and this is the signification of the word "remainest". It is not exactly His essential and eternal existence, but it is that, while associated with that which passes away, He abides. The truth is that while His hands had made these things, that He was their Creator, and, by and by, He will "fold them up and they shall be changed", He is "the same". His years fail not.

But He is no distant Deity, no disinterested spectator of anything His hands have made. He regulates as truly as He created. If, for some good reason He sees fit to dissolve His handiwork, He has most certainly the perfect right, as well as the power, to do so. Yet He Himself remains! And, if so, shall not His continuance be the guarantee of something greater and better—of a new heaven and a new earth wherein dwelleth righteousness? That He remains is the hope of that creation of God of which He is "the beginning" (Revelation 3:14).

Hence His all-sufficiency. He can both build and destroy and then build again. He can occupy every moral sphere and fill every spiritual vacuum. In Him all fullness dwells. He who was in the form of God and thought it no robbery to be equal with God, assumed, in wondrous grace, the form of a servant and the fashion of a man. Such was the extent of His incarnation. He was an actual man, like ourselves in all things except sin, leading a true and perfect human life—a Man amongst men, in order to present God to us as He, the Son eternal, only could, and win our confidence toward God if such a thing could be done, but going down to death, so as to annul its power, remove its sting and gain a glorious victory over it—"death, even the death of the cross!"

Mark the stages in His condescension. From Godhead to manhood, thence to servitude, thence to death, and that (oh grace inconceivable!) the death of the cross—the most ignominious, agonizing, shameful death of all! Well may we sing:—

> "We love Thee for the glorious worth
> Which in Thyself we see,
> We love Thee for that shameful cross
> Endured so patiently."

But He is risen from the dead and highly exalted. We can sing: "Thou remainest." He "remaineth" in view of a ruined creation, and He remaineth in view of a disintegrated church. He is the hope of both and "the bright and morning star" of His assembly. He is her all-sufficiency—her resource, her centre to-day, as at all times. He is "the same" in days Laodicean as He was in those of Ephesus. He is God's "Amen" to-day, maintaining, in undiminished power, all the counsel and purpose of God, spite of the fearful drop from the bright apostolic period to the present nauseous condition of the church's faithless testimony. He is on the wrong side of the door of the profession of His name; so that He urges the purchasing of gold and clothing and eye salve, to expel its dross, and cover its nakedness, and enlighten its blindness. Outside He knocks, and seeks admission to the willing heart; for spite of the church's palpable degradation, He "remaineth" as "the Same".

Conditions may possibly change outwardly, and "difficult times" characterize these closing days, but He changeth not. And hence the second Epistle to Timothy, foretelling as it does these very days, presents to us, not so much the House of God as a well-ordered system, but Christ Himself as the foundation which stands steady, be the collapse of Christendom what it is. "Remember", it tells us, "Jesus Christ ... raised from the dead." He remains as the HEAD; let us hold it fast; as LORD, let us obey His word; as the only CENTRE of gathering, let us gather to His all-sufficient name; as the still REJECTED CHRIST, let us humbly cleave to Him and His cross; as the soon-coming BRIDEGROOM, let our hearts, in all the glowing affections of a faithful bride cry: "Even so, come, Lord Jesus."

He "remaineth" as THE HOPE OF ISRAEL—the nation of His choice and favour—but long driven out of its land, scattered, peeled, persecuted because of its sins, but never forgotten of Him, but rather "beloved for the fathers' sakes", to whom the promise of earthly blessing was made. The Deliverer will yet "come out of Zion and turn away ungodliness from Jacob", and reinstate the nation in the Land promised it of old. For "the gifts and calling of God are without repentance" (see Romans 11).

Then, finally, if we descend to the necessities and cares of the individual Christian, can we not say that when all else is gone, the hopes dashed, the chair vacant, the poor feeble heart crushed, the eye dimmed with tears, and the soul desolated by waves of sorrow, He remaineth the Comforter, the resource, the peace-giver, the abiding Friend, who Himself proved, in deep and true experience, all the sorrows of our pilgrim path, so that He is able to succour and sympathize with us.

That He remaineth "the same yesterday, to-day, and forever", may not be the highest of His many glories, but it is not the smallest of those great dignities which make His sacred name precious to His saints in all generations—as their dwelling place, their hope, their refuge, their power and their victory.

As such, how worthy He is of all our gratitude, thanksgiving and praise. That pen is made of gold which writes of Him; the ministry which has the all-sufficiency of the Lord Jesus Christ, whether as Saviour, Lord, or Head of His body, for its primary theme is assuredly the ministry of the Spirit of God. His own closing command was: "Believe also in Me"—given just ere He went to the Father, suggesting, as it does, all that is contained in the fact that He remaineth.

If that be true no change of passing conditions need agitate the spirit of His people, or affect the steady labour of His servants. His grace will not fail.

God's Present Ministry

IT seems to me that, in a gracious superiority to all the petty conflicts and jarring voices of the day, the Spirit of God continues to unfold the glories of the Lord Jesus Christ to the hearts of His blood-bought people everywhere. For this is ever His ministry. "He shall take of Mine" (said our Lord in John 16), "and shall show it unto you." This ministry proceeds throughout the centuries, be they dark or bright; and, in thus bearing witness to our rejected Master, the Spirit of God works continuously. He will not be hindered by the power of sin or Satan. He is God. Now this is full of encouragement, and happy it is, in days admittedly dark and difficult, to trace His working, and to discover that the enemy is far from having things all his own way.

We are too prone, alas, to regard the triumph of evil and get under its power. This is depressing. It is not faith in God, but the result of looking at things seen and temporal with consequent feebleness.

"We walk by faith, not by sight" (2 Corinthians 5), and God would have us regard "the work of His hand", and in so doing be strengthened. Now there is no question in the minds of those who have taken the trouble to appraise events, that during late years there has been an unprecedented ministry of Christ, both as to the value of His death and resurrection, and also of His personal glories, whether as Son of God or Son of Man. He has been the theme and subject-matter, as never since apostolic times, of His more intelligent servants everywhere. Christ has been preached with a fullness unknown for long, and this, it is needless to say, is the direct and blessed work of the Spirit of God.

That He was loved and cherished, and followed by many a faithful heart through ages dark and cruel, we can easily trace. The page of history sparkles with the devoted lives and martyr-deaths of hosts to whom Christ was more precious than all things here. Of these the world was not worthy. They paved the way amid the darkness of their surroundings for the light which shines on us to-day—a light so little appreciated!

The glorious Reformation (so called) was that work of God which drew universal attention to the work of Christ, and of our justification by faith thereby. This poured a perfect flood of light over the face of Christendom, and made the Word of God a new Book to countless numbers. It was the dawn of a holy liberty, and a death-blow to the corruptions of Rome. But what need to hold fast that which we have! What need to stand fast in that liberty and to hold to the Word of God! But then, is our liberty everything? Can we feed on our own personal emancipation alone? Does the knowledge of justification (however precious) suffice for the soul? Has God no further revelation?

He has! What is redemption without the Redeemer, or salvation without the Saviour? What is the servant without his Lord; or the church without its Head?

Nay, what is Christianity without that Christ who, on ascending to the right hand of God, sent down the Holy Ghost to baptize into one body all who believed the gospel, and to be the power of life and testimony in the saints till Christ shall take all hence to be for ever with Himself in the Father's House?

Absolutely nothing! As well have the solar system without the great and all essential orb of day. This were impossible. "A pleasant thing it is to behold the sun", and a far greater pleasure it is for the saints of God to hear of the deep, boundless glories of His eternal Son!

I am bold to say that these glories have been, and are, the specific testimony of the Spirit of God during the last and undoubtedly closing years of this dispensation. The best wine comes last although contained in the original "firkin". The Word of God has His Son for the highest theme.

Nor do I doubt that this ministry is having the present effect of reuniting at least the hearts of great numbers of saints who see in it something beyond traditions and mere ecclesiasticism, something that will eventually bind their hearts and minds and tongues together in common and eternal adoration in heaven.

Pity, a thousand times over, that such adoration should be broken up into fragments to-day by the unhappy "shibboleths" and warring factions into which the church is now divided! But, thank God, to-day will quickly pass, and then and for ever one all-commanding Object will fill our gaze, and bring about that concentration on Himself, who is the One Shepherd of the one flock and the Head of the one body, which in our every heart we so ardently desire, and which, amid other things, He died to accomplish.

He "died for our sins" indeed, but, notice, He also "died to gather together in one the children of God which were scattered abroad"; and the fulfilment of this is certain. That unity is bound to be brought about; only may each of us seek, in his prayers, and ways and associations, to give personal effect to it now.

How cheering, how stimulating the truth! This is, most assuredly, part—and a very great part—of the ministry of the Spirit of God to-day.

Christ the Creator

THAT which gives special interest to "creation" is that, in Scripture, it is attributed to Christ—the Lord.

No doubt, speaking in the abstract, it is viewed as the work of God, and so we read in Genesis 1:1, that "in the beginning God created the heavens and the earth", but in the same chapter (verse 26) it is said, in sacred colloquy, "let us make man", indicating co-operation on the part of the Holy and omnipotent Godhead; for each Person in the Godhead is God; and, hence, in the creation of the highest creature on earth, we find a consultation between those Persons, which was not taken in the production of any lower part of it. Man was created in the image and likeness of God, and was placed in sovereignty over all His works.

"God created!" Let that formal statement be clearly apprehended. There was, and there is what Scripture calls "creation". There is "the whole creation" and its "beginning" (2 Peter 3). The fact is stated with the utmost simplicity and with a naturalness that bespeaks absolute truth. No lengthened explanation, no wordy elaboration to meet the incredulity of man is given.

The thing itself is so inconceivable, that no other solution is possible but that "God created". That profound, but entirely satisfactory record, suffices for faith, and is, at once, the simplest and the only key to "creation". It is "by faith we understand that the worlds were framed by the word of God." Speculation and cosmogonies may fade in this light.

Very well, creation is the work of the Godhead, but, in particular, it is that of the Second Person, as the Scriptures, when giving assignment, invariably declare. And therefore, if that be so, the work of creation, in its omnipotence, its design, its intricacy, its minuteness, its continuance, its perfection, becomes to the Christian a matter of deepest interest. Our Lord Jesus Christ is Creator! Wondrous fact indeed, but when cordially admitted, the further and much greater work of redemption becomes more glorious in our estimation; for, if every detail in the former were perfect, how could a flaw or defect be found in the latter? A perfect Creator is also a perfect Redeemer, and vice versâ as well.

These two facts are placed in juxtaposition in Colossians 1:15-18, "For by Him [the Son of God] were all things created that are in heaven and in earth", and not only created "by Him", but "for Him"—a most significant statement surely, and one which throws creation into an extraordinary place of importance, viz., for the special purpose and enjoyment of the Son of God—the Christ; and again: "He is before all things", necessarily so, if "by Him they were created"; and, lastly, "by Him all things consist." They subsist, they are maintained in existence by His power and will. These "all things" depend, both for their origin and support, on the will and pleasure of the Son of God.

CHRIST THE CREATOR

He is also, as risen from the dead, Head of the body, the church—the Redeemer—pre-eminent in all things. The same two facts present themselves to us in Hebrews 1 and 2; we read in chapter 1:10, "And thou, Lord, in the beginning [mark that word] hast laid the foundation of the earth, and the heavens are the work of Thine hands"—hands of the universal Creator; while, in chapter 2:10, we find Him qualified through sufferings to be the Leader of His people's salvation, and also their Deliverer from the fear of death by having annulled the power of the devil. Blessed Saviour! Or, again, in chapter 1:3, He who upholds all things by the word of His power, has made expiation for the sins of His people, and has sat down on the right hand of the majesty on high. What rich qualifications are His! Finally, if in John 1 He is seen as the Lamb of God—the sin-bearer, so too is He revealed as God—the Word—by whom were all things made, and without Him was not anything made that was made. He was indispensable in creation from beginning to end; and when He shall fold up, as a vesture, all that He had made—change it, and cause it to perish, He, withal, shall remain, and prove Himself to be "the same"—"the everlasting God, the Creator of the ends of the earth", and the worthy Co-Recipient of the glad homage of "every creature in Heaven and on earth and under the earth and in the sea", as they ascribe "Blessing and honour and glory and power to Him that sitteth upon the throne and unto the Lamb for ever and ever"—

> The power of earth's Creator
>   Gives glory to Thy Name.
> The love of earth's Redeemer
>   Enhances still thy fame.
> Creator and Redeemer
>   Almighty Saviour! Lord,
> The power and grace that saved us
>   For ever be adored.

"A Saviour, Jesus"

ONE of the most resplendent crowns which shall rest on the head of our Lord Jesus Christ is that of Saviour. Beside His name none other is given under heaven whereby men must be saved (Acts 4:12), and so we read: "He that believeth on Him is not condemned: but he that believeth not is condemned already, because he hath not believed in the name of the only begotten Son of God" (John 3:18). The refusal of His name is fatal. We may well thank God for that name as we remember how that He "so loved the world as to give His only begotten Son, that whosoever believeth in Him should not perish, but have everlasting life" (John 3:16). May we lay hold of the fact that the heart of God the Father is the fountain-head of the river of saving grace; thence it flows in measureless fullness over a world alienated from God, so that all and any who are conscious of their lost condition may, by faith in His Son, become the recipients, here and now, of all that grace can give—possessors of everlasting life! But this grace must reach us on grounds of absolute righteousness. The throne itself would be outraged were its just claims not perfectly met and satisfied; and seeing that this could never be accomplished by the creature already powerless and guilty, it must be rendered by One fully competent to do so.

"A SAVIOUR, JESUS"

Him we find in the Son of God! He is the divinely provided ransom. God Himself has provided a lamb for a burnt-offering. Here, then, we start. This is our foundation; it is solid and sure, and clean outside all that is of man. We can freely speak of a Saviour-God! He loved and He gave, and the given One came willingly to do all that was charged upon Him. But if this should be on the side of God, what is there on that of man? There is, alas! only the sin that necessitated grace so boundless.

Sin? Yes. And what is sin? Its nature is questioned to-day. It is vainly explained away; but none the less it remains in its undiminished virulence and universality. Neither has philosophy, nor civilization, nor education, nor science, nor any human device that the clever brain of man has invented, removed sin from the heart, or its dire consequence of death, and the grave, and the judgment beyond, from the race of fallen, guilty men. There it is, as patent and potent to-day as ever; so that he who denies it is blind, or worse.

Let us get on to this bed-rock truth, else salvation means nothing and a Saviour is a mere sentiment.

God declares that "all the world is guilty before Him" (Romans 3:19), that it "lieth in wickedness" (1 John 5:19), and that "Satan deceiveth the whole world" (Revelation 12:9). The cross was its moral judgment (John 12:31). So much for the mass; but, personally, "all have sinned, and come short of the glory of God." The power and poison of sin are rampant in every department of life, in every sphere and circle and bosom. These vast cemeteries bear mighty witness. "Death has passed on all men, for that all have sinned" (Romans 5:12).

What, then, is sin? It may be seen in a thousand aggravated and sickening forms, from murder to a thought of foolishness (Mark 7:21-22); but notice, "the movement of a heart in opposition to the will of God is sin." Who can escape here?

Hence the Lord said to certain accusers, "Let him that is *without sin* first cast a stone at her" (John 8:7). Needless to say no hand dare cast a stone. Every man was guilty of some sin; none was, nor is, nor can be "without sin".

The crying need of the day is a true sense of sin, and therefore of humiliation and repentance before God. Always so, but perhaps more truly now than ever; and if so, woe to those who minimize the gravity of sin and its certain and eternal judgment.

This clears the way for God's salvation. And what is that? Nay, who is that? It is Christ Himself! "Mine eyes have seen Thy salvation", said Simeon as he held the infant Redeemer in his arms.

Never can that salvation be understood until it is seen to be embodied in the person of our Lord Jesus Christ, as dead, and risen, and glorified.

His death was necessary for expiation, and His blood alone, but fully, can cleanse from sin.

His resurrection from the dead was also necessary as proof of the work of atonement done, and no more sacrifice required. By one offering He hath perfected for ever them that are sanctified (Hebrews 10:14).

And His ascension was necessary, that He might send down the Holy Spirit to give effect to His work, and seal for eternal blessing the souls of all who believe. Oh, lay hold of the deep meaning of the words *"one offering"*. Let that offering stand before your eye in its absolute all-sufficiency. Think who it was that was offered! Remember the cup He drank and the curse He bore! Ponder the love

"A SAVIOUR, JESUS"

that led Him into such fathomless depths! View Him as the sinless Son of Man who obeyed to the letter, and who alone glorified God where all else had failed! Smite your breast as you behold the sight of Calvary! Learn the love of Christ that passeth knowledge! See the whole awful question of your sins and sin, your guilt and state, settled in His death, so that you, delivered from every thrall and fear, at cost so infinite, might love Him in return, and serve and follow and worship Him, until, by His side, you see the crown of your salvation on His glorious brow for ever.

The Angels and the Magi

IS it not remarkable that, in comparing the two chapters (Matthew 2 and Luke 2) which give us an account of the earliest days on earth of our Lord, we find that the effect produced by the angelic announcement of His birth in Luke 2 was very small? It appears not to have affected the people of Jerusalem in the least.

The shepherds abiding in the fields, keeping watch over their flocks by night, were the immediate recipients of that wonderful communication from heaven.

Having heard the message of the angel of the Lord—"Unto you is born this day in the City of David a Saviour which is Christ the Lord"—they heard also a multitude of the heavenly host praising God and saying, "Glory to God in the highest, and on earth peace, good will towards men", and were so stirred in heart as to go at once to Bethlehem in order to see the thing which the Lord had made known to them. They saw, and made known abroad the saying which was told them concerning this child. They published it generally.

Never had child been born under such auspices, nor introduced by such angelic acclamation, but their declaration was unnoticed. The wonderful saying which the shepherds made known abroad fell on ears dull and apathetic. The public effect was nil. No one appeared to care.

Shepherds! Who would listen to them! They were poor ignorant men, visionaries of some wild delusion. Had the priests and the scribes carried the report there might have been some reason in hearing it. But shepherds—announcing a Saviour born that day, even Christ the Lord, and He, too, lying in a manger—impossible, incredible, and only to be ignored.

The story was so unlikely! A Saviour, the Christ, Jehovah, born and lying, forsooth! in the manger of some cattle-shed, swaddled there in circumstances of palpable poverty! Never! A palace would be too mean for such a one! The highest dignities that earth could proffer would be unworthy of the Christ, the Saviour; but that Saviour, the Lord, Jehovah, cradled in a feeding-trough staggers conception.

Yes, the mystery of the grace of the Incarnation has always done so. Nature and reason stand bewildered. The story is either true or false. It is either the greatest act of humiliation (save, indeed, the cross) or the wildest piece of imagination that ever entered, or could enter, the brain of man. Indeed, such an invention is utterly inconceivable.

Ten thousand thanks be to God, the Manger of Bethlehem, ennobled by the presence, in infant form, of Christ the Lord, stands out in all the certainty of a fact divinely attested, and accredited by faith!

But in spite of the common indifference, we find some Simeons, and Annas, and others, even in Jerusalem, who were in expectation of redemption. Anna spake of the Redeemer to all such, and Simeon took Him into his arms, and blessed God that he had now seen His salvation.

Thus we see that the hearts of a few (alas, that there should have been so few!) were prepared to welcome the Lord. But so ever. God has wrought by minorities all along the line and made them His vessels of testimony and triumph. Study these minorities; there are many of them. Consider Noah and his seven; Gideon and his three hundred; Daniel and his three; Paul almost alone. Such minorities saved (as we say) the situation. God uses vessels that lean on Him; and such was the remnant of whom we are speaking, be they poor and unlettered shepherds, or people but little known to the world around them. "The secret of the Lord", we read, "is with them that fear Him; and He will show them His covenant" (Psalm 25:14). So in this case.

But when, a year or more afterwards, there came wise men from the east (Matthew 2) to inquire in Jerusalem for the King who had been born, guided as they were by a star which mysteriously, silently, but surely announced His birth, "Herod", we read, "was troubled, and all Jerusalem with Him."

The advent of a Saviour, proclaimed as it was by the hosts of heaven, created little or no interest, but that of a King—one born as such—in distinct rivalry to Herod and his superior, the Roman Emperor, caused trouble everywhere.

The messengers were but men—their guide a star; their nationality Gentile; and yet with credentials so meagre their testimony was universally accepted. They were reputed, Gentiles albeit, as wise men, astrologers—Magi—men who read the heavens and their portents. These, therefore, were witnesses far more reliable than illiterate shepherds would be; and so their message told. The city was troubled, from the King downwards. "Where is He", they asked, "who is born King of the Jews?" King, and only King, was their statement. Saviour and Lord they know not. The star signalized only a King—where is He?

Herod, fearful of his rival, appealed to the scribes for help. They turned to the Scriptures—that infallible guide, when truly understood, to eternal facts which are beyond the ray of a star, or the conception of man.

"Bethlehem", said the scribes; "for thus it is written by the prophet, 'And thou Bethlehem art not the least among the princes of Juda, for out of thee shall come a Governor that shall rule My people Israel' " (Micah 5:2). Thus did these scribes quote the prophet; they mentioned the "Governor", but they saw fit to leave out the wonderful words which follow: "whose goings forth have been from everlasting", (or, as it is in the margin "from the days of eternity"). They concealed the fact that this King was the Lord, Jehovah!

The wise men proceed to Bethlehem, being again led by the star, and coming to the house to which they are directed, they find the young child and Mary, His mother, and present to Him their treasures—gold, frankincense, and myrrh. They fall down and worship Him.

But being warned of God as to the cruel intentions of Herod, they depart to their own country by another way. Their visit had caused disquietude and trouble in the city. Such was its effect. No King but Cæsar was wanted there, least of all that King who had been born at Bethlehem, whose goings had been "from the days of eternity." And so Herod, the mere creature of Cæsar, wreaks vengeance on all the children of Bethlehem from two years old and under, hoping to destroy his rival "King".

That King had, however, been carried to Egypt, and not only placed there beyond the power of Herod, but that another Scripture should have its fulfilment—otherwise impossible—viz., "Out of Egypt have I called my Son" (*cf.* Hosea 11:1). Ponder the words. The Son of God called out of Egypt suggests the beginning of a totally new history for Jew and Gentile, on the proven and utter breakdown of both before God. The Saviour—Christ the Lord, of Luke 2, is the blessed Son of Matthew 2. The Saviour is the King, and the Saviour-King is also Jehovah and Son of God. Wonderful harmonies, truly!

"Never Man Spake Like This Man"

John 7.

NEVER! This encomium was absolutely true!

Officers had been sent by the chief priests in Jerusalem to take this wonderful Speaker, and bring Him to them from the Temple, where He had been boldly stating His mission, whence He came, and who He was; but the statement was so pronounced, so definite, so unequivocal, that, envious as they were of His fame, and fearful of His rivalry, they could devise no other plan of silencing Him than by force. Hence the charge given to the officers.

They went, intending, doubtless, to obey the orders of their masters, but before attempting to apprehend Him, they listened to His words and became deeply interested. They heard Him say to the unbelieving crowd: "Ye shall seek me and shall not find me, and where I go ye cannot come." These words, no doubt, struck them: they announced a Personality and opened out a wisdom and a superiority to circumstances, which at once placed Him, in their minds, above the level of ordinary speakers. Here was one who knew clearly what He was about, who spoke with calm authority and proclaimed an independence unknown to others. He thus asserted a right to speak and to command the hearing of all. Had such another speaker ever been heard in the Temple? Never.

What man was this? Needless to ask, for He had just made a sufferer of thirty and eight long years perfectly whole; and who could do that but God? That lowly Man who thus spoke in the Temple under the frown and threat of Jerusalem's rulers was in fact their promised Messiah—Son of Man and Son of God. His mighty works proved His Person.

No wonder that the officers were fascinated! Instead of finding a noisy declaimer of Roman or other government, they were brought face to face with a speaker so calm, so dignified, so uncompromising and yet so bold, that they were more than overawed. They felt themselves powerless to carry out their orders. The superiority of that presence, the majesty of that Person, forced them into admiration of Him. Further, they heard Him say: "If any man thirst let him come unto Me and drink … out of his belly shall flow rivers of living water."

"If any man thirst"—and who, in this weary world, does not thirst? A universal thirst is proved by a universal discontent. That word is written big in the bosom of every individual of every class and nation on the face of the earth—a thirst that nothing can slake but this wonderful "living water" given by the Son of God. There is to be found, as many have proved, an abiding satisfaction that leads them to eschew the overtures of a world that can never satisfy.

"If any man thirst let him come unto Me and drink." That is all; but the result is glorious, for he shall not only be personally satisfied, but rivers of living water shall flow from him for the refreshment of this weary, barren, hopeless world. What a miracle, but how true, as the blessing of these two thousand years has proved!

"Come unto Me and drink"—that is all. But the secret is in that "*Me*."

No religious festival can slake this thirst—the thirst returns, as we can testify.

No service, no ordinance, no priesthood, no imposition of hands, no human benediction, no power of man nor angel can give the "living water" which satisfies for ever. They who drink thereof are "born, not of blood, nor of the will of the flesh, nor of the will of man, but of God." They come, as thus born, to the Son of God. They drink, they are satisfied, they become channels of wide and generous blessing to all around. Again, what a miracle!

And whoever had, before, heard such words?

It was the voice of Him who, on another day, said to His captors: "I am He"—words so uttered that they who heard them went backward and fell to the ground; but not so here. His voice which by and by "shall shake not the earth only but also heaven", but on this occasion His accents were those of grace and mercy and compassion for the thirsting souls of men.

The officers returned alone to their masters, who at once said to them: "Why have ye not brought Him?"

They could assign no reason. He made no resistance, nor did His followers, and yet bring Him they could not. All they could say was in this truest of all confessions: "Never man spake like this man."

They thus admitted that they had been overcome by His words themselves. They were "spirit and life"; and, their inherent and resistless power restrained them from carrying out their mission. His hour had not yet come.

"Are ye also deceived?" replied the Pharisees; "have any of the rulers believed in Him?" Impossible that any but the ignorant could do that.

Not a single ruler? Yes, one, and Nicodemus speaks out, who, in the shades of night, had heard the words of the lowly Speaker, had been spellbound by them, and had been drawn from his darkness into a knowledge of the love of God in the gift of His Son, of the substitutionary work of the Son when lifted up on the cross, and of eternal life through faith in Him.

To Nicodemus, as to the officers, "never man spake like this man"—no, nor acted, nor moved, nor suffered, nor sympathized, nor loved, nor died, nor was raised by the glory of the Father to be Saviour, Lord and Head like this Man, and to receive in heaven eternal adoration from myriads of worshippers, who are indebted to Him for the work He did, and the words He spoke.

"Jesus Wept"

THERE was sorrow in Bethany, death had entered one of its houses—the only one, in all probability, where the Lord found a welcome—and had removed a dearly-loved brother. Hearts were crushed and broken. A very tender tie had been snapped and mourning had taken the place of joy.

"Why this blow?" might have been the unspoken language of the two bereaved and desolate sisters. Had the Lord only been there, they felt sure that their brother would not have died. He, who loved all three, would have spared them the sorrow through which they had passed. His healing power had been so often shown that, had He only come in time, this disaster might have been prevented.

Now, however, it was too late. The Lord had allowed, for some inexplicable reason, known to Himself alone, the precious days to slip away; and when, in an apparently tardy response to their message, He had come at last, not only had death done its work, but the dead one was buried. Surely the Master had failed, on this occasion, in the display of the sympathy which was one of His most lovely traits.

How little did the sisters know the deep meaning of that delay. It was not occasioned by lack of love, or care, or consideration, but by a vastly superior motive, viz., "the glory of God, that the Son of God might be glorified thereby"—the glory of God and of His Son, our Lord Jesus Christ, is the supreme object in the universe. Everything must subserve the glory of God—Father, Son and Spirit; and, to this undivided glory, the proud or fearful, or self-seeking heart of man must bow, and, in bowing, find rest and peace and assurance.

He who walked in the light of day knew exactly when to take His journey back into Judea, and to Bethany and its broken hearts.

He who said: "I am the resurrection and the life" was quite as able to raise one from a four days' state of death as He was to prevent him from dying. He who had just given eyesight to a man who had been born blind could certainly have caused that even Lazarus should not have died.

But there was to accrue to the Son of God a greater glory than that. He was to be seen as the giver of life, not now to the gentle child of Jairus, who had just expired; nor to the only son of Nain's widow, who was being carried to his grave, but to one whose body was already yielding to corruption and had become putrescent. The glory of God is all-various in its working, but it has the welfare of His creatures as one of its objects.

The glory of the Son of God was seen in His absolute obedience to the Father's will; but, while expressing itself in the raising of the dead, and the bestowing of life, and life eternal too, it proved itself in the exhibition of the fullest, tenderest, human sympathy.

"JESUS WEPT"

Did He not suffer in order that He might fill the place of High Priest, and, as such, minister timely help and strength and comfort to His needy dependent, sorrowing people here? Most assuredly!

See, then, when He had found His way to the grave, and had witnessed the dire effects of death on the bleeding hearts around, we read ... and, let the words of this, the shortest and perhaps, the most profoundly significant, verse in our Bible, sink deeply into our memories: "JESUS WEPT!"

He wept who was "the resurrection and the life"! He wept who possessed all the power of God and the warmest sympathy of man. Yes, "Jesus wept." He who was ever in the form of God is seen here in that of a servant. His service was one of love.

On that sympathy we can always count, for He is "the same yesterday, to-day, and for ever."

> "Jesus wept! those tears of sorrow
>   Are a legacy of love;
> Yesterday, to-day, to-morrow,
>   He the same doth ever prove:
> Thou art all in all to me,
> Weeping One of Bethany."

And recently hearts innumerable have been torn, crushed and bleeding. Loved ones have fallen on fields of battle. Desolation has covered the face of the earth. Each country has shed its tears; on all hands there are widows, orphans, sisters, parents, brothers and friends who have mourned and wept. But behind the inscrutable wisdom that has allowed a convulsion so awful, there is, at the same time, a gracious and sympathetic support richly ministered by the ascended Lord who gives the assurance that, if the one He loved may not be restored, as was Lazarus, yet He says: "Thy brother shall rise again", for in the fullest sense "whosoever liveth and believeth in Me shall never die." That is, there is no death, as such, for the Christian. He is "absent from the body and present with the Lord." Death is annulled for such; while on the other hand, "he that believeth on Me, though he were dead, yet shall he live", for "life and incorruptibility are brought to light by the gospel."

Here we may find our richest consolation. Can you picture a more lovely sight than the sacred Weeper of Bethany? There He stands, at the grave-side in moral touch with its mourners, not in a spirit of cold superiority as might have become death's victor, nor even in the aloofness of Him by whom all things were made, but in the full pathos of One who, while Creator and Sustainer of all, cherished a heart of tender human pity.

We repeat the words: "Jesus wept." May I ask the afflicted and sorrowing if they can find no comfort in those tears, no solace in that sympathy, no Friend that sticketh closer than a brother in this best of all friends, no compensation in His love, no pillow for the heavy head, no resting-place on His puissant arm, no one to occupy the empty chambers of the stricken heart—One better than the best and dearer than the dearest? What a triumph for faith when HE is thus known and loved!

It gives glory to the Son of God when the bereaved and broken heart finds all its satisfaction in Him. He will be everything to us in our bright eternity, and this He may be in our present but brief period of sorrow and loss.

The Son of God

"He saith unto them, But whom say ye that I am? And Simon Peter answered and said, Thou art the Christ, the Son of the living God."—Matthew 16:15-16.

THE significance of this question put by the blessed Lord to His disciples must be apparent to the reader. At that moment a crisis had been reached in His testimony, by the only too evident refusal thereof on the part of the leaders of the nation. He had come to "His own", and, now, in the panorama of His life, as presented in this first Gospel, we see that "His own received Him not."

He had been announced by the Baptist, the herald of the kingdom, in terms of charming interest; and the wise men had been attracted from the east by the finger of God to do Him homage. He had proclaimed in the mountain, the holy principles of the kingdom; He had wrought miracles of mercy on every hand; He had bidden the weary to find rest in Himself—the Son of the Father; He had, as Son of man on earth, pardoned sins; He had, as the promised Messiah, opened the eyes of the blind; He had been owned as Son of God by Satan, whom as "the strong man" He had bound, and, as the stronger, was able to spoil his goods; but, withal, He had been proudly rejected, even where His greatest works had been done. There was no national repentance. This sin and that of His rejection went together.

As to the common opinion regarding Him, He might have been John the Baptist, or Elias, or Jeremias, or one of the prophets: that was all! Unconcern, on this vital point, marked the mass. This "greater than Solomon", both in wisdom and works, was ignored. He was despised and they esteemed Him not. Nevertheless, it was their Messiah whom they thus rejected. How blind, how culpable they!

Then it was that He asked of His disciples the question: "But whom say ye that I am?" He could surely count on some hearts which would respond to it, for there must ever, in days the darkest, be those in whose hearts God is working, for He never leaves Himself without witness; and accordingly Peter made answer: "Thou art the Christ [the Messiah] the Son of the living God."

But this rich and true confession was by no means the fruit of the natural mind. Such knowledge does not originate in the heart of man. It was communicated to Peter, said the Lord, by "My Father which is in heaven." It was necessarily a direct revelation.

But there it stands, in its eternal value, to command the faith of every one who professes the name of Christ. Let the words "the Son of the living God" carry their due weight with every believing heart and conscience, and call forth the adoration that is meet.

"Whom say ye that I am?" Not only Jesus of Nazareth; nor alone the Christ known to us on high, seated, as Man, on the throne of the Father, Head over all things to the Church, which is His body, but as "Son of the living God", over whom death had no power, nor could it hold

Him. May this supreme glory of His infinitely glorious Person engage the attention of His saints increasingly. Let us remember that we live in a day when that Person is, in one way or another, disparaged.

The holiness of His humanity is denied on one hand, and the truth of His deity is assailed on the other; but, in this question and answer, "whom say ye that I *the Son of man* am", and "Thou art the Christ, *the Son of the living God*", we have both facts stated as equally true—"the Son of man" and "the Son of God". Hence it becomes us to cherish both His perfect manhood and His essential deity. And it may be very fairly questioned if He can be worshipped aright, unless this relationship be owned. My soul, dost thou truly recognize in thy once dying Redeemer, who bought and washed thee from thy ten thousand sins in His blood, the veritable Son of God? If so, then prostrate thyself at His feet, and magnify, adore, and worship Him.

When on the Mount of the Transfiguration, Peter, James, and John were privileged to hear the voice from out of the cloud saying, "this is My beloved Son, hear Him." That voice Peter never forgot: nay, "we have not followed cunningly devised fables," he wrote (in his second epistle) "when we made known unto you the power and coming of our Lord Jesus Christ, but were eye-witnesses of His majesty." He received an indelible impress of the glory of our Lord as the beloved Son on the Mount, even though, in his written ministry, he treats more of "the Christ" than "the Son".

James early earned a martyr's crown (Acts chapter 12), so that we have no ministry from his pen: but the writings of John are replete with the moral glories of "the only begotten Son, which is in the bosom of the Father." And how we love those writings! How they enrich and call forth the adoration of the soul!

Then, if we refer to Paul, we find that his very first text in the Damascene synagogue, as soon as the scales had fallen from his eyes, was that "Jesus is the Son of God!"

This was the first note of his lovely song—the first tribute to the glory of Christ in his testimony. It formed the backbone of all the rest. Hence the extraordinary and Spirit-owned (as Spirit-given) power of his ministry. That ministry was manifold; it covered the Gospel as it had been made known, in a special way, to him; and then he writes of Jesus being "declared to be Son of God with power ... by resurrection from the dead", so that not only the resurrection of our Lord, but His deity as well, give colour and character to the apostle's gospel (see Romans 1:4).

So, too, it covers his ministry of the Church; for in his Epistle to the Ephesians, in which he treats of the Church as the present vessel of the grace and purpose of God, he speaks of the gifts of the ascended Christ, as having for their object "the perfecting of the saints, the work of the ministry, the edifying of the body of Christ: till we all come to the unity of the faith, and of the knowledge of the Son of God, unto a perfect man, unto the measure of the stature of the fullness of Christ" (Ephesians 4:12-13).

Here the knowledge of the Son of God is the acme of all spiritual attainment, and the grand object of the Spirit of God in the edification of the body of Christ. "Whom say ye that I am?" is still the great question for heart and conscience. That knowledge is clearly the deepest and most profound, as well as the initial, in the whole revelation of God: for, on the glory of His person the value of His atoning work depends. The issues for eternity, whether as regards glory or judgment, depend on the person and work of the Son of God.

Along with the knowledge of the Son is that of the Father, and this is "eternal life" in its full Christian or present aspect, even as we shall, when in glory with the Lord, enjoy it in absolute fulness for ever.

May the Spirit of God give us fresh unfoldings of the Son of God day by day.

A Word to the Weary

LET me quote the verse from which these words are taken: "The Lord God hath given Me the tongue of the learned [the instructed] that I should know how to speak a word in season to him that is weary" (Isaiah 50:4).

1st. WHO SPEAKS THE WORD IN SEASON?

Who is that "Me" who is instructed by the Lord God for a service so precious and so deeply needed?

It is He who (as the same passage states) asks the question: "Is My hand shortened at all, that it cannot redeem? or have I no power to deliver? ... I clothe the heavens with blackness, and I make sackcloth their covering."

In His hand is all that power. He can redeem; He can deliver; He can darken the face of the sky; in His hand is omnipotence—a truly wonderful Person is He!

And yet He it is who is qualified to do a service so infinitesimal as to drop a word of comfort into the ear of the weary. What vast extremes are in His service!

He who covers the heavens can comfort a poor weary heart here below. And He does!

2ND. HOW DID HE ACQUIRE THIS ABILITY?

How, in what school, did He receive this learning? How comes He to act in sympathy and to feel the sorrows of His afflicted people? The answer is given us in Hebrews 2 and 5. There we read that He "took part in flesh and blood"; He became incarnate; He stooped from Godhead glory into the fashion of Man; as man He learned obedience by the things which He suffered. He who had hitherto commanded, who "spake and it was done", now learns obedience in suffering, as each of the four divinely-given biographies of His perfect life makes known to us; it was in this school—that of weariness and weeping, of hunger and poverty, of contact with every phase of human misery and woe, the tears of the doubly bereft widow and the desolated home of Bethany, the painfully visible effects of sin and the groan of a convulsed creation—in this familiar school and not in the unruffled dignities of heaven He learned the art, rare and precious, of sympathy and of speaking a word to the weary. His sympathy is the result of dearly-bought experience, and is, therefore, ever efficacious.

He is touched with the feeling of our infirmities. "He was tempted in all [note the word] points like as we are, yet without sin"—i.e., sin wholly absent.

3RD. THE WORD SPOKEN IS SEASONABLE.

His word to the weary is spoken, we read, *"in season"*. That is, He knows the exact moment when to whisper into the wearied ear, and just when to support the breaking heart.

It was in a moment of physical crisis in my own career, that I learned the meaning of His rod and staff comforting me. I had, till then, attached the idea of support to that staff. Now, I discovered that there was also "comfort". So says the charming pastoral psalm, where we find the sheep drifting down through the valley, but, even there, comforted by the shepherd's rod and staff! Yes, but this makes the dreaded valley a very easy journey when you find that such comfort is yours in it, and that beyond its shadow is the House of the Lord for ever!

Christ's ministry is always seasonable, never out of season. It may not assume an audible form, as it oft-times did in days of old, as, for instance, to Abraham, Moses, the prophets, or to Paul, once and again, but in some sweet and suitable way by the Word, or otherwise—a psalm, a hymn, or a spiritual song—the patient service and comfort of the living Lord, is proved by the weary.

4TH. WHO ARE THE WEARY?

Well, such a question is superfluous to-day. … Who is not weary?

"And they shall be weary. Thus far are the words of Jeremiah" (chapter 51:64)—a striking statement at the close of this significant prophecy, but not very dissimilar from the "groan" of Romans 8. Wearying and groaning are, did we only allow the fact, the chief features of humanity to-day. The frivolity of nature can only be accounted for by its insensibility. The awful fact is that "the god of this world hath blinded the minds of them that believe not", and this diabolic obfuscation of mind, on the part of all such, is the reason of this sad phenomenon. Did everyone feel as he should that he "must give account of himself to God", how different would be his thoughts and habits! But "God is not in all his thoughts", and hence the trifling.

But not so is the weary. To him God is real, and needed, and obeyed, and loved. He follows in the blessed steps of his Master and Lord. He realizes the contradiction to God on all hands. He is oft-times weary, rightly so, and he it is who receives and enjoys "a word in season" from Him who has power to redeem and to deliver, as well as to cover the heavens with blackness, or do what He will in the armies of heaven.

> "Thy sympathy how precious!
> Thou succourest in sorrow."

"Jesus the Son of God"

THESE words stand out bold and clear as a statement of the Spirit of God which allows no kind of qualification. They bind together the humanity and the deity of our Lord. They present, in blessed union, His lowly name as Man and His divine title as God.

Their setting is exquisite. We read in Hebrews 4:14: "Seeing then that we have a great high priest, which is passed into the heavens, Jesus the Son of God, let us hold fast our profession."

The enormous difficulty of maintaining the Christian profession, in power, is only too well known by the true believer. He has a profound sense of his own spiritual weakness and tendency to yield to the foe, so that he values, all the more, the care and support, the sympathy and succour of our Great High Priest, who hast left us in an adverse world, has passed through the heavens, where, none the less, He sustains us in the path of faith, and who comforts us in all the tribulation of our heavenward journey. He is possessed of all power. We are to make a constant use of the throne of grace, in order to receive, thence, the grace and mercy needed for each and every exigency and trial. We may connect the mercy with the name of Jesus, and the power with the Son of God.

A wonderful combination of words are these: "Jesus the Son of God"! It is not "Jesus the Saviour of sinners", nor "Jesus the Christ", nor "Jesus the Head of His body the church", but "Jesus the Son of God". He comes before us in Deity.

But this dignity had already been noted of Him in the first chapter of this epistle. There we read that God has spoken to us by the Son (in Son); that He is the brightness of His person; that He upholds all things; that He made expiation by Himself, and then sat down on high; that He receives the worship of angels; that He is saluted as God; that He created all things, and will, by and by, cause them to pass away, while He remains the same. He is God the Son as well as Son of God, Creator and Sustainer of all things. This prepares us for our Spirit-given phrase: "Jesus the Son of God".

How glorious His priesthood! How able is He to carry His people through, and how full of encouragement to them to hold fast their profession. He met their sins by expiation; He meets their infirmities by priesthood; but, whether in the work of expiation or in the execution of priesthood, it is in each case "Jesus the Son of God". For God He always was, and God and Man He ever remains.

I need hardly say, however, that this Epistle to the Hebrews is not the only scripture which, in definite terms, declares His deity. If, in an ordinary biography, the writer happened to state, but once, that his subject was a scion of nobility, the reader would unquestionably accord him that distinction; but if the writer repeated the same statement and gave, at the same time, varied and incidental proofs of it, all uncertainty would be removed from the mind of the reader.

Further, if other and separate biographers, who, on account of the distance of time could not possibly have written their different books together, stated the same fact, then, surely, there could be no room for disbelief. "At the mouth of two or three witnesses every word shall be established."

First, in the very earliest chapter of Genesis we have an intimation of the plurality of the Persons in the Godhead. "Let us", we read, "make man in our image, after our likeness". The statement is significant even though we are not given anything beyond the fact of plurality. But, here and there in the Old Testament, which rather teaches the unity of the Godhead than its trinity, we discover the existence of those three divine Persons who are explicitly, and purposely, and fully revealed to us in the New Testament.

If we turn to Psalm 110, spoken "by the Holy Ghost" (Mark 12:36), we find the words: "The *Lord* said unto my Lord, Sit Thou on My right hand"; in Micah 5:2: "A Ruler in Israel; whose goings forth have been of old, from everlasting"; in Zechariah 13:7: "My Shepherd ... My fellow, saith the Lord of hosts".

In the pages of the New Testament the declaration is full. To acknowledge it is highest bliss; to deny it is fearful sin; only how necessary it is to apprehend the Godhead of our Lord Jesus Christ, as indeed His manhood in its essential sinlessness, in a spirit of becoming reverence and lowly grace. Controversy thereon should be eschewed, and the simple and yet majestic truth accepted. Reason is beggared here. Revelation is worthy of the highest exercise of reason, and that is faith in what God has declared. For nothing is so rational as faith in God. "Jesus the Son of

"JESUS THE SON OF GOD"

God" must be allowed to stand before the bowed and adoring heart, in all the dignity, glory, majesty, and deity, of His Person as "God manifest in flesh".

In the close of the Gospel by Matthew we have the formula of Christian baptism. It is to be in the name of "the Father, Son, and Holy Ghost"—the Godhead in Trinity, and each Person is to receive equal honour in this initial rite. The dignity of Each is the same, as is the honour to be accorded. It will be remembered that, in the synoptic Gospels, the accounts of the baptism of Jesus are practically similar. "My beloved Son" is the salutation of the Father in each. In the Son the Father had found His pleasure. So in the Transfiguration, He was again spoken of as the beloved Son, and was to be heard as such. It is still "Jesus the Son of God".

The fourth Gospel introduces Him in deity—"The Word was God"! But the same Word "became flesh"—a brief, decisive statement of what we call the "Incarnation"— and, as such, He dwelt among us "full", thank God, "of grace and truth"; and, as "the only-begotten Son, which is [mark the word—it signifies subsisting there ever, and that as Son] in the bosom of the Father, He hath declared Him." How complete! Who but the Son of that bosom could adequately declare or express the Father? None but He! And so, in chapter 10, He affirmed that He and the Father were one. In chapter 8 He pronounced the eternity of His existence in saying: "Before Abraham was I am." Later on, Thomas confessed Him as both Lord and God.

Passing on to Paul, once the inveterate hater of the name of Jesus, the very first thing he did after conversion was to preach in the synagogues: "Jesus, that He is the Son of God" (Acts 9:20, R.V.), and this initial text was only developed and emphasized during the course of his

Christian ministry; for the Christ he ministered as Saviour, Lord, and Head of the church was also "the Son of God who loved him and gave Himself for him"—"God manifest in flesh"—"over all, God blessed for ever." His highest theme was the deity of Jesus.

Then Peter in his second epistle tells how he had been an eye-witness of the magnificence (is the word) of the Lord Jesus as seen on the holy mount, when he actually heard the voice of God the Father saying: "This is My beloved Son in whom I am well pleased." Hence, to him, after such a vision, the glory of Christ, and His coming kingdom, was no "cunningly devised fable". It was a mighty and all-controlling fact.

Finally, John, in closing his general epistle, says: "We know that the Son of God is come ... and we are in Him that is true. This is the true God and eternal life."

Thus the deity of our blessed Lord and Saviour Jesus Christ is abundantly confirmed throughout the length and breadth of the Word of God. Such is the Great High Priest of our profession.

Christ our Pattern

THE Christian is enjoined to follow the steps of Christ. He is not commanded to speak as He did of whom it was said: "Never man spake like this man" (John 7:46); nor to do the works of Him who said: "If I had not done among them the works that none other man did" (15:24), for, both in words and works, He held a place absolutely pre-eminent. He was the truth, and all He said was infallibly true. He "went about doing good, for God was with Him", and miracles of mercy followed where He went.

The Christian is not commanded to do miracles, like his Lord, but he is exhorted to *"follow His steps"* (1 Peter 2:21). This he is bound to do. It is his duty and pleasure to trace out his Master's footsteps and to place his own feet in them. This is the truest form of discipleship.

Let it be very clearly understood, however, that no one can imitate the Lord Jesus Christ until he is consciously reconciled to God on the ground of redemption. The imitation of Christ on the part of one who has never been "born again", nor, therefore, a child of God, is impossible. The attempt must be a total failure; and the more honest that attempt the greater will be the disappointment. It were a thousand times easier to paint the rainbow on canvas than for man, as such, to exhibit in his life the moral features of Christ.

No, a man must have not only new desires, but a new nature and a new power, that of the Spirit of God, who alone can so minister Christ to the renewed heart that it seeks His image and also conformity to it.

It is by the Spirit of the Lord that such an one is "changed into the same image from glory to glory" (2 Corinthians 3:18). And may I say that no change is so complete and exquisite as this.

Think, for instance, of a Saul of Tarsus—the chief sinner, changed into the image of the Lord Jesus!

Think of the same change being effected in any of us who have learned our natural loathsomeness—that we should bear that image—fully in the glory itself, but gradually and increasingly now while on our journey to it! What a wondrous power this supposes; but, just as surely as the Spirit of God dwells in the believer, so does this process of sanctification proceed, though assuredly not to the eye of the believer himself. Others can notice the progress of the Christian as he moves on "from glory to glory". He becomes more like his Pattern. Wonderful fact! Nor will the process cease until he shall be "conformed to the image of the Son, that He may be the first-born among many brethren." They shall remember Him who shall be the Chief of all.

"Christ also suffered for us"—there He stood alone, for none but He could take our place under the judgment due, nor exhaust its awful sentence, when He was "made sin for us"; but beside making atonement in death, "He left us an example that we should follow His steps." Here

He is not alone. Not one of His loved and blood-bought people but should follow His steps.

Some may follow them more faithfully and closely than others, but He tells us that His "sheep hear His voice, that He knows them, and that they follow Him." This is the one distinguishing mark of all His sheep. They follow Him.

It is remarkable that the word "example" here, is found nowhere else. It means a "copy or underwriting". It is not the same as that of the Apostle when he charged the saints at Philippi to be followers together of him and "to mark them which walk, so as ye have us for an ensample"; nor again when he urged his son Timothy to be "an example of believers". In these cases it is a "type", but here it is a "copy". That is, our Lord Jesus Christ is the standard, and no lower one will do.

Can we, then, reach this standard here below? Certainly not; but still, "Every man that hath this hope in Him [the hope of being like Him when He shall appear] purifieth himself even as He is pure" (1 John 3:3). Again, we have the universality of the process. "Every man" addresses himself to reach that perfect Standard.

Needless to say that He holds a place far beyond the reach of man. He is "the true God and eternal life" (1 John 5:20); but here we are dealing with the standard of purification and the Pattern—the copy for our imitation. Men speak of high ideals; could any ideal exceed this?

And what are the steps we are to follow? They are to be traced from the time when, in the midst of the doctors, He said: "Wist ye not that I must be about My Father's business?" to that when, that business perfectly completed, He cried: "It is finished", bowing His blessed head and giving up His Spirit to the hands of His Father.

What a study! What an example! Our passage in 1 Peter gives us a summary of the steps in four bold negative statements:—

1. "Who did no sin."
2. "Neither was guile found in His mouth."
3. "Who, when He was reviled, reviled not again."
4. "When He suffered He threatened not."

Mark, in these He left us an example; and how we are rebuked as we view Him absolutely clear of the failures to which, alas, we are all so prone.

And then, in deepest confidence, "He committed Himself to Him who judgeth righteously." If the other statements presented His life negatively this gives us the constant repose of His soul in a positive way. His vindication was of God. Are we in the habit of making this committal? We gain a victory when we do so; for there the battle ends. His whole life was submission, hearty and unquestioning, to the will of the Father. This was His yoke. It was easy. And when we, through grace, bow unmurmuringly to that will, we, too, prove the yoke to be easy and the burden light.

But there must be reality. The headline must be copied, and the example imitated. The most beautiful (only beautiful) steps have been imprinted on this more than desert waste, by the holy and sacred feet of the Son of God, leaving behind them the plainly visible signs of the one path that is pleasing to God, and that which, in the power of the Holy Spirit, each and every child of His should pursue.

CHRIST OUR PATTERN

> "The Lord is Himself gone before,
> He has marked out the path that we tread.
> It's as sure as the love we adore,
> We have nothing to fear nor to dread.
>
> "There is but that one in the waste
> Which His footsteps have marked as His own,
> And we follow in diligent haste
> To the place where He's put on His crown."

Yes, He has gone on high. We behold with unveiled face His glory there. Every ray of it is lovely; it wins the heart; it separates from earth; it changes him who beholds into "the same image from glory to glory as by the Spirit of the Lord." The transformation is marvellous but divinely simple. The Potter fashions the vessel as it seems good to Him, and the skill of the Potter is seen in His work.

Beloved, may we set our hearts on acquiring a much greater likeness to the Lord Jesus Christ who is our Pattern as well as our most precious Saviour.

The Cross of Christ

THE cross of Christ is, beyond all comparison, the most wonderful fact in the universe—the most beautiful in its display of perfect love, but the most hideous in its expression of human enmity and wickedness. It is the meeting-place of the grace of God and the guilt of man. There these two opposing forces came into direct collision. There we see God and there we see man, fallen man. There we see, not only the love of God to man, but we learn His justice in dealing with evil—His righteousness in the treatment of the sin that could not have otherwise been atoned for, but in the death, under divine judgment, of the holy, spotless Son of God—the willing victim of Calvary.

Let it be seen that, in order to vindicate His character, and to clear His throne of the possible charge of complicity with sin, it was necessary that God should deal with that awful question in a way so judicial that it might be settled, finally and definitely, to the silencing of every accusing voice for ever. The flood had only done so in measure, loud though its protest was. The victims slain on Jewish altars, though types of a greater sacrifice, "could never put away sin."

Nay, a Victim of infinite value alone could meet the infinite demerit of sin, "The Son of man must [note the word] be lifted up." The payment must equal the debt, and the amends must be commensurate with the penalty. Who can pay the penalty? Neither man nor angel! The Son of God alone!

Now, mark, if infinite demerit demands an infinite substitution, it follows that the substitution refused—that is, Christ rejected, then infinite—that is, eternal judgment is the necessary alternative. Terrible fact!

It is either acceptance by faith of the substitionary death of the Son of God, and full salvation; or the heartless rejection of Him and eternal punishment—one or other. Thank God that "the blood of Jesus Christ, His Son, cleanseth from all sin"; but to tread that blood under foot is to incur a doom sorer than "death without mercy". Who can face such a doom? But, in the cross, God's righteousness is declared as fully in the equitable justification of the believer, as is shall be in the condemnation of the sinner.

He is "just and the justifier of him that believeth in Jesus." Hence the glorious moral value of that wondrous cross! Unless its voice be heard and understood the soul can never really know God. Then, why is the cross so proudly shunned, or why should it be a stumbling block? Just because it is the fullest exposure of man. It condemns him root and branch. It shows that his very "righteousnesses are as filthy rags", and that the whole world is running in opposition to God, saying by its triple condemnation of Christ, "Crucify Him", "crucify Him", spite of its polished letters in "Hebrew, Greek and Latin". Therefore your attitude towards the cross determines your relation toward God. You cannot esteem the cross if you love that which it condemns. If you "love the world you are an enemy of God."

But this thorough exposure of man in his lost condition and hatred of God is only one aspect of the cross of Christ. The other is God's perfect way, in purest grace, of meeting the whole question of sin, wherever its poison may have spread, and of carrying blessing to man in his deepest guilt. Divine and glorious solution!

God incarnate becomes the willing victim in order to expiate sin by being "made a curse for us"! Could any conception be more marvellous? And so we read in Colossians 1 that it is by "the blood of His cross" that all things in heaven and on earth (but only there) are to be reconciled; and thus, He, whose precious blood was shed thereon, shall be seen as "the Lamb of God" who taketh away, in its vast and vile entirety, "the sin of the world."

No miracle like the cross of Christ! Then, if the cross be of such value to God, what is it to His children? Can anything surpass its worth? They who witnessed it "smote their breasts". The Roman centurion exclaimed: "Truly this man was the Son of God." The sweet story of Calvary has captivated the hearts of myriads, and turned them from sin and Satan to God and life eternal; while the courts of heaven re-echo the notes of praise for ever. There is no fascination like this wondrous cross. The world may bewitch, and by its allurements enslave its votaries, but:—

> In Thy cross I saw a beauty
>   Far outshining all I knew,
> There Thy love's surpassing lustre
>   Won my heart, and bound me too.
> Now, oh! Lord my heart is spell-bound,
>   Not, as once, by earth's vain blaze,
> Calvary's cross, eternal Lover,
>   Charms and fascinates my gaze.

The Risen Lord

"Why seek ye the living among the dead?"—Luke 24:5.

THERE they stood at the edge of the empty sepulchre—a group of true-hearted but perplexed and disconsolate women!

They had brought, at early morn, ere the busy world was astir, their already prepared spices and ointments.

But the tomb where the body of their Lord had been laid was empty; hence their bewilderment.

They had seen Him in death, and had marked "how His body was laid." But what now? That body was gone—how, where?

As they were much perplexed thereabout, two men stood by them in shining garments, who said to them, "Why seek ye Him that liveth among the dead?" (Luke 24:5, margin).

"Him that liveth"! What could that mean to these downcast women? He whom they sought was not there, but was risen! The sepulchre was empty; the spices and ointments were useless; but if He were alive again, the power of death had been broken, together with all that could signify.

A living, risen Christ—that is the starting-post of vital Christianity! Christ risen from the dead, having annulled the power of death and the grave, having broken the power of Satan and made atonement for sin—that is its mighty foundation!

"He is risen"—that is our pæan of victory! "Him that liveth"—that is our everlasting strength and consolation!

Now see the immediate effect on these very women. We read that "they came and held him by the feet and worshipped Him" (Matthew 28:9). Their perplexity gave place to worship, and their desolate hearts were filled with gladness.

"Rabboni", cried the weeping Mary, when she heard Him call her by name.

"My Lord and my God", said the unbelieving Thomas, when generously invited to thrust his hand into the spear-riven side.

"The disciples", too "were glad when they saw the Lord" (see John 20).

Oh! it was the dawn of a new day, the beginning of a new creation, the closing up of types and shadows, the presence of the glorious Antitype in actual resurrection form, visible, tangible, accessible, gracious as of old, and exactly "the same" as "yesterday", when He wept and suffered and sympathized, and as, thank God, He will be "for ever". The blessed Leader of Salvation had been made perfect—thoroughly fitted and qualified by suffering—for His new place as such.

THE RISEN LORD

See the effect on Stephen, the lovely proto-martyr of Christianity. He was full of the Holy Ghost who had been sent down by the living, risen Christ after His ascension to heaven, and consequently, in the power of this glorious indwelling Spirit, he cried: "I see the heavens opened and the Son of Man standing at the right hand of God"! (Acts 7).

What a vision! But how thoroughly in order.

We know the sequel; he was stoned to death, but passed away in deepest peace, saying, like Him on whose face he was gazing, "Lord, lay not this sin to their charge." He "fell asleep" like a wearied child rocked in its cradle. Death was, as we said, annulled, shorn of its sting and terror. See the effect on John in Revelation 1. He had fallen prostrate in the visible presence of the Son of Man, as He walked, judicially, amid the seven golden candlesticks. There he lay, but on him was laid a gentle hand, while a well-known voice said: "Fear not, I am He that liveth and became dead, and behold I am alive for evermore"!

Enough; fear fled, the seer arose, the apocalypse followed full of terror to the world, full of comfort to the true and faithful church.

It is still the risen, living, and coming Christ.

Notice, "Because I live, ye shall live also", are His precious words in John 14. With Him we are "in safeguard", indeed, as David told one of his trembling followers.

As certainly as He lives on the other side of death, so shall each and all of His beloved and believing people. For He is their life. Hence we read in Hebrews 7:25: "He ever liveth to make intercession for us." Such is the present activity of His life in glory—our High Priest and Intercessor.

"He that keepeth Israel shall neither slumber nor sleep."

Oh! there is succour, sympathy, care, consideration, love in that tender heart up there on the throne! He has felt our pangs; He has shed our tears; He has known our sorrows; He was made like us in all things but sin; He calls us His brethren. He is the star and sun of the Christian life!

A creed, a rule, a form, a system, a kingdom, a heaven! Oh, more, infinitely more is our living, loving, tender, holy, faithful Lord! It is everlasting life!

No marvel that Paul could write of and crave for "the surpassingness of the knowledge of Christ Jesus, my Lord." It surpasses and eclipses all beside.

This knowledge is no fable, nor myth, nor imagination.

The Christ of God and of Christianity is a living Person—truly God and truly Man—the Son of the Father, the Redeemer of men, the risen, glorified Lord and Head of the church, who appeared once to put away sin by His own sacrifice, who is coming shortly to call His own to be for ever with Him in the Father's house—those whom He loves to the end, and who will appear again in judgment and power and glory.

Beloved, it is ours to-day, during His rejection, to learn His personal worth—to set our hearts on this one thing, so that we may bear the stamp of Christ upon us in the reproduction, in our poor frail bodies, of His beautiful life of love and holiness. This is the truest fruitfulness and greatest joy. Let us bathe our souls in the pure waters of John 14, 15, and 16, until we can better appreciate John 17.

> "Lord Jesus, make Thyself to me,
> A living, bright reality."

Christ's Priesthood

"We have not an high priest that cannot be touched with the feeling of our infirmities."—Hebrews 4:15.

IT is only in the Epistle to the Hebrews that Christ is definitely spoken of as Priest—"the High Priest of our profession"; but, if intercession belong to that office, as it surely does, we read in Romans 8:34: "It is Christ that died, yea rather, that is risen again, who is even at the right hand of God, who also maketh intercession for us."

Mark, His intercession is His present exercise in heaven, as the result of His death and resurrection. These, completed to the glory of God and the settled peace before Him of all who believe (in present justification and filial relationship), furnish the ground of this precious intercession—of Priesthood.

By no means does intercession add to our security as believers. That is assured already; nor does it move the heart of God toward us, as though we needed reconciliation. "For if, when we were enemies, we were reconciled to God by the death of His Son, much more, being reconciled, we shall be saved by His life" (Romans 5:10). The death of the Son of God, sent of the Father in infinite love, effected our complete reconciliation; the life of that

Son, in present glory and power, secures our salvation from every menace.

We start our Christian course as reconciled, and made secure for ever, by that which has been done for us in the death and resurrection of the blessed Lord; but we have to pursue that course in conscious weakness and dependence. We need an arm on which to lean and a heart as faithful as it is kind in which to confide day by day.

This we have fully in our great high Priest. His intercession is active for us before God; and His succour and sympathy are continually realized by His tried and tempted people here below.

If the Spirit makes intercession in us with groanings which cannot be uttered, so does our faithful Lord intercede for us on high.

Little we know how indebted we are for those intercessions!

Little did Peter appreciate that his Master was praying for him, so that, when the temptation came, his faith should not fail; or how that intercession was answered when, having failed, he "wept bitterly". His faith, thus, was kept in life, though, in order to learn his lack of dependence, he himself was allowed to fail.

"If any man sin," we read in 1 John 2, "we have an advocate with the Father, Jesus Christ the righteous."

It is advocacy with "the Father" because relationship is supposed, and confession is made to the Father on the part of the offending child, so that his offence is forgiven, and he is "cleansed from all unrighteousness." Advocacy is therefore subsequent to intercession. This is for sustainment, that is for restoration, so that communion may be full and unclouded. Advocacy is distinct from intercession, which properly has to say not to sin or failure, but to infirmity and need.

Hence we are told to "come boldly unto the throne of grace, that we may obtain mercy [pity] and find grace for timely help" (Hebrews 4:16). A more lovely expression could not be found for the tried and needy pilgrim than "the throne of grace". It signifies the omnipotence of compassion—pity all powerful!

The words are derived, I gather, from chapters 1 and 2. In chapter 1, having made expiation, Christ sits down on the right hand of the Majesty on high; while in chapter 2, He is presented as a merciful and faithful high Priest. Hence we may speak of a mercy that is majestic, and of grace enthroned! And all this for those who feel their own personal inability for one step of the way.

Is not such living compassion predicated in John 13-17? We have the feet washed in 13; "another Comforter" in chapter 14; slavery exchanged for friendship in chapter 15; "good cheer" in face of a hostile world in chapter 16; and the most wonderful intercession in chapter 17. Surely we may discover all this in the present priesthood of our Lord. And were not His "learning obedience" when here below, His "strong crying and tears", and His death itself His qualifications for that office? Did He not reach perfection by the things He suffered? He alone can best sympathize who has passed through the sorrow; and so we read of His being a "Man of sorrows" before we read of His soul being made "an offering for sin" (Isaiah 53). His perfect life as Man preceded His expiatory death on the cross. Now He is highly exalted. "We have such an high Priest, who is set on the right hand of the throne of the Majesty in the heavens" (Hebrews 8:1). Nor did He glorify Himself to be made an high Priest. That He did not, but the title lay in the unique dignity of His person: "He that said unto Him, Thou art My Son, to-day have I begotten Thee", said also, "Thou art a Priest for ever after the order of Melchisedec" (Hebrews 5:5-6). His title lay in His personal glory as Son of God; His qualifications lay in the sore ordeal of His perfect life of sorrow among those who had proved the bitterness of the results of sin in its myriad forms. He was apart from sin, but not from tears, nor hunger, nor thirst, nor weariness. He went into death itself to complete His path of perfect obedience, and, at the same time, to atone for sin, and to overcome all the adverse power of Satan.

He is free now to exercise, in the place of divine power, the functions of a merciful and faithful high Priest toward all who come unto God by Him. He ever liveth to intercede for them, and is able to save them to the uttermost—for ever!

All thanks and glory to Him!

"The Coming of the Lord Draweth Nigh"

NOW that the church is rapidly nearing the Home-call and the longed-for moment, when the Lord will fulfill His promise of coming again and receiving us to Himself, so that where He is we may be also, does it not become us to raise our thoughts and enlarge our expectations in view of the mighty translation that must be so near at hand?

"Hope deferred", we read, "maketh the heart sick", and there is more than the possibility of that sickness so depressing the spirit that hands begin to hang down, and knees to become feeble.

Not, however, that the Lord delayeth His coming; for, what seems long to us is not so to Him, to whom a thousand years are only a day; but as time is the great test of endurance, so, as weary years drag on, we become impatient and ready to droop. So it was with Israel in Egypt when the deliverance expected at the hand of Moses failed to reach the suffering people as quickly as they had hoped. But the mills of God, in grinding slowly, did their work on Pharaoh in His own good time, if not in that of Israel.

So, again, when the people had lost sight of their leader when receiving the "lively oracles" on the fiery mount, becoming impatient, prepared to return to Egypt, saying, "As for this Moses we wot not what is become of him", the sickness of deferred hope had stricken them.

For a like impatience of spirit, King Saul forfeited his crown.

The loss of patience and of hope is the sign of coming collapse; and against such a thing we, to-day, must contend.

Never was a day so truly full of hope; never was the coming of the Lord so near; never, throughout these dreary centuries, was there a time when, with yearning hearts turned heavenward, the church of God, as a concrete whole, should be looking thence for the Saviour—the longed-for Deliverer—to accomplish, in a moment, that glorious translation, according to the power (a wonderful power indeed) whereby He is able to subdue all things unto Himself (Philippians 3).

Let our earnest gaze be heavenward while our hearts, more than ever, await their divinely implanted craving of seeing Him face to face.

> "How will our eyes to see His face delight,
> Whose love has cheered us thro' the darksome night."

Oh! but the night has been dark and drear, and the road steep and long, and the bride of His heart is weary and travel-stained! She feels His absence; she longs for Himself; she finds no home here below; she pants for the ineffable joys of the Father's House—its rest, its comfort, its love and light; its full unison of heart and hand; its sacred circle undivided for ever; its immunity from every form of evil, its unfettered enjoyment of full spiritual

"THE COMING OF THE LORD DRAWETH NIGH"

power in such worship as shall be to the glory of the Father and the Son for ever!

Gladsome prospect!

But is the longing all on her side? No, no, most surely not. It is stronger far on His.

Consider His closing words to her as He says, "I am the bright and Morning Star"—herald of day and of Home!

A star so long hidden from view by the shades of night, breaks at length in the distant sky to cheer the weary watcher and tell him that his vigil is over. That star is the star of morning! The night and its testing is past; no need for patience and hope now.

> "The eye at last beholdeth
> What the heart hath loved so long."

The expectation is gratified; the heart is at rest. And that star calls Himself a "bright" star!

But why "bright"?

Just in order to place Himself in contrast with the signal failure of that profession of His holy name which has, alas, sunk down from its pristine power and separation to God (as we see in the Acts of the Apostles) to a condition so nauseous that it has to be utterly ejected, as we read in the address to Laodicea.

Whilst He remains "bright", the profession has dropped into fearful moral pollutions until He can only describe it as wretched, blind, and naked.

To this profession He is nothing but the Judge, and it is doubly guilty before Him; but to the bride He appears, at the soon coming close of her long and tremulous vigil, as the Star of the Morning, as bright and glorious and unchanged as ever!

How bright her prospect; how bright her hope; how bright the Star of that hope!

To Him "the Spirit and the bride say 'come.' " And our hope, so long deferred, will, very soon, give place to sight, and our feeble faith to glad fruition.

Meanwhile, as the shore is nearing, and the perils of the voyage are almost over, may we say the one to the other, "Be of good cheer, for I believe God that it shall be even as it was told me."

"Let not your heart be troubled ... I will come again."

The Bridegroom

"He that hath the bride is the bridegroom"—John 3:29.

THE Bridegroom's possession of the bride is absolute and exclusive, for the relationship is inviolate, none may interfere.

Other ideas may present themselves, those of fitness and affection, but this is the chief. The bride is the absolute and inalienable property and possession of the bridegroom. And such possession carries its own peculiar joy to his heart. He sees in her an helpmeet for himself, his counterpart, his intelligent and loving co-partner who can not only share his joys and sorrows, but who feels that they are her own. Union produces identification, there is perfect community of interest, there is full reciprocity of wish and action, and that on account of the existing union between the two.

Now, Christ is presented, amid other relations, as the Bridegroom, and the church—not the individual saint— is spoken of as His bride, His wife. Given to Him of the Father, purchased by His precious blood, and the object of His special affection, she is His peculiar property, and belongs to Him alone. She is, *par excellence*, "His own". He loves her to the end. As in the case of ordinary marriage a man shall leave his father and mother, the otherwise strongest of links, and shall cleave unto his wife. For this is the original institution as ordained by the Creator, and intended by Him to be maintained in all the sacredness of the tie. It is under His authority as Creator, and is to be disregarded at the peril of the offender. He shall "cleave unto his wife". This was the divine decree in the brief day of innocence, when discord was unknown; it is the decree of God to-day, when sin, alas! has created such a host of difficulties, but when, at the same time, grace is well able to make the tie as strong and tender as at first. Oh! how admirably does Christ make good His part in this mystic union. How true and tender, how patient and faithful is He!

Now, as to the reality of this relationship let us look first at Matthew 22. There we read of a certain King who made a marriage for His Son, and who sent forth His servants to call them that were bidden to the wedding. This is, no doubt, the gospel-call. The servants are sent out to invite to a wedding. They share in the joy of the King and of His Son. They are in that exquisite secret. They have before them not only the happiness of the guests, but they have the gladness of the Bridegroom. He is a poor evangelist (it may be said in passing) who has only the good of the sinner before him. To have that is well, but to have the joy of Christ in His coming nuptial day is far better. Let us realize the value of souls increasingly, but let us also have that day clearly in view, and think of the pleasure that the Son shall have when He shall survey His fair and glorious bride "unblemished in His sight". This is a wondrous stimulus to the servant in his oft-weary labour, viz., that he can beget such joy to his Lord. The grand object of the gospel should fill his heart with its infinite gratification to Christ.

THE BRIDEGROOM

Then in Matthew 25 we have the "midnight cry" which awakens all the sleepers, wise and foolish alike, and leads, consequently, to the definite and final separation of the two companies from each other. That cry is, "Behold the Bridegroom." It implies His advent no doubt, but attention is drawn, not so much to that, as to Himself—the one commanding theme of the Spirit of God.

Of the bride nothing is said here, for all interest centres in the Bridegroom, and it is the preaching of the Lord Jesus Christ, in whatsoever character or glory, that produces the greatest effect and leaves the deepest impression.

Elsewhere it is, "Behold the Lamb of God which taketh away the sin of the world"; or only, "Behold the Lamb of God"; or again, "Behold the Man." Here it is, "Behold the Bridegroom!" And at length He comes, and they that are ready go in with Him to the marriage—to the moment of His joy—and the door is shut. "Even so, come, Lord Jesus!"

Now let us learn from 2 Corinthians 11 the sanctifying power of this truth: "I am jealous over you", says the Apostle Paul, "with a godly jealousy, for I have espoused you to one husband, that I may present you as a chaste virgin to Christ."

This beautiful simile is in keeping with all that has preceded. Paul had the grand design of the gospel before him—the marriage of the King's Son. His consuming desire was to present the church all pure and chaste, detached in heart and life from the snares of Satan and the power of evil, to Christ, as to "one husband". He laboured for fidelity on her part to the rightful claims of this one Husband that she might respond, in all her ways, creditably to such a relationship. Could any appeal be more affecting? He saw the seductions around, and he pleaded for the exercise of those sacred affections which should ever burn in the bosom of the faithful bride, and express themselves in her conduct.

Then Ephesians 5:27-32 gives us the result in the presentation to Himself of that church which Christ not only gave Himself for, but which He also sanctified and cleansed, with such infinite patience all her journey through, that she is seen at last "glorious, not having spot or wrinkle or any such thing, but holy and without blemish." It is the bride that is here depicted. She is seen to be the product of the work of Christ from the cross right on to the day of presentation. To Him she owes all her beauty.

We pass on to Revelation 19:7-9, to "the marriage of the Lamb"—the consummation of all! "His wife", we read, "hath made herself ready; and to her was granted that she should be arrayed in fine linen, clean and white, for the fine linen is the righteousnesses of the saints." She is credited with such, and is granted thus to be arrayed—pure and bright, and made ready for the nuptial day. The joy on each side is complete.

Then a thousand years pass away, and she is seen in the figure of a city (Revelation 21:2-24), descending out of heaven from God, but still prepared as a bride adorned for her husband. Time leaves no scar; the wrinkle once effaced, never returns; the bridal beauty remains. The city is resplendent, the glory of God lightens it, and the Lamb is the light thereof. Defilement is excluded for evermore. Glorious prospect!

Arise, Thou bright Morning Star, bright Herald of the day, and touch the chord which will cause "the Spirit and the bride" to say, in deep and rich union, "Come" to Thyself; the longed-for heavenly Bridegroom—Thou

THE BRIDEGROOM

"conspicuous among myriads"—Thou "altogether lovely" who hast won the affections of these myriads by a love which, for them, has passed through death's dark waters and sin's heavy judgment, and which lives on to-day and for ever; nor shall it rest until Thy blood-bought bride is with Thee in eternal glory. Again, "Even so come, Lord Jesus."

> "From the dateless timeless periods,
>   He has loved us without cause,
> And for all His blood-bought myriads
>   His is love that knows no pause.
>   Matchless Lover!
>   Changeless as the eternal laws."

The Coming King

WE find in Scripture that God deigned frequently to reach the attention of people by means of dreams. Many instances could be adduced. Now, however, we have in the Scriptures the full unfolding of His mind, so that dreams, having that for their object, are unnecessary. There is enough in the Book of God to give complete intelligence to every willing heart as to all that is connected with our spiritual well-being for time and eternity, as well, surely, as to very much more than our personal well-being.

If people only knew the value of the Bible, they would prize it much more.

A mighty king of Chaldea, Nebuchadnezzar by name, had a wonderful dream. He saw, in vision, an image—great, excellent, terrible! It stood before him. Its head was fine gold; its breast and arms were of silver; its belly and thighs of brass; its legs of iron, and its feet part of iron and part of clay!

There it stood—silent, mysterious, significant!

Such a statue, composed of material so heterogeneous, had never been unveiled to mortal vision before.

No ordinary dream this, and none of the wise men of Babylon could relieve the affrighted monarch of the terror of that dream.

God had sent it, and God alone could explain it to him.

He who sent the dream fitted and sent the man to give the explanation.

Daniel, the devoted, godly captive, was entrusted with the dream and the key. Giving all credit to God, he told the king the wonderful secret—a secret of the ages!

Would that the politicians, and the statesmen, and the rulers of to-day would attend to the disclosure of this ancient dream!

An image of gold, silver, brass, iron and clay: these are four kingdoms, coming in succession—from the gold of that day to the incoherent iron and clay of our own. It is easy to see them—Babylon, Persia, Greece, and Rome—the last being protracted, and its influence being felt universally to-day.

There stood that image, whose form was terrible, containing such elements of wealth and power, such stores of gold and of iron! How puissant, how resistless! No wonder the king was troubled, or that "his sleep brake from him" (Daniel 2:1).

Such a problem must be worked out. But, notice most carefully, we read: "Thou sawest till that a stone was cut out without hands, which smote the image upon his feet … and brake them to pieces. Then was the iron, the clay, the brass, the silver, and the gold, broken to pieces together, and became like the chaff of the summer threshing-floors; and the wind carried them away, that no place was found for them: and the stone which smote the image became a great mountain, and filled the whole earth" (Daniel 2:34-35).

That was the greatest wonder of all! What could this mysterious stone, cut out without hands, be?

The image was smitten, ground to powder, and displaced by the stone. Marvellous stone! It becomes a mountain and fills the whole earth! The chaff of the threshing-floor is replaced by the stone which smote the image.

Yes, ye politicians, and statesmen, and empire-makers, who are engaged in tasks so enormous and so complex, and for which ye are sacrificing time, talent, brain, muscle, fame, and fortune, see ye not that ye are but building together that which shall become the chaff of the summer threshing-floors, while there is suspended overhead the Stone which is bound to pulverize your gigantic labours and bring them all to dust?

Mark:—"In the days of these kings shall the God of heaven set up a kingdom, which shall never be destroyed: ... but it shall break in pieces and consume all these kingdoms, and it shall stand for ever" (Daniel 2:44).

When?

When the kingdom in mystery, as known to-day, shall give place to the kingdom in might—then!

To-day the kingdom of God is in moral and spiritual power; soon it will be in visible actuality.

To-day the church awaits her Lord for the meeting in the air at His coming. Thereafter the Stone shall fall, and grind, and crush to powder, as, like a mountain, it fills the whole earth, and "the kingdoms of this world become the kingdoms of our Lord and of His Christ" (Revelation 11:15).

He is wise who devotes his attention, not to "the chaff of the threshing-floor", but to the Stone, and the kingdom, and the King. For, as surely as "the gold" of Babylon has passed away and its place can hardly be discovered, so shall "the iron and the clay" of the present moment be dissolved as well. These kingdoms are evanescent, God's kingdom shall stand for ever.

The King, hidden to-day in heaven because of His rejection and death here, is made known now in richest grace as Son of God and Saviour, Advocate and Great High Priest, Head too of His body the church, but soon to appear with her in glory; and then, as the Stone cut out without hands, but introduced and established by the power of God, to reign in absolute monarchy and in perfect wisdom, power, and righteousness.

Such a King and such a kingdom have never yet been known; but, as certainly as "the chaff of the threshing-floors" shall be swept away, so shall this mighty Stone fill the whole earth and "stand for ever."

King of Kings

"KING of kings" and "Lord of lords"—
O how rich these glorious words!
Titles high and boundless fame
Now enhance the Saviour's name.

Him who once was crowned with thorn,
Crowns of glory now adorn;
Jesus sits upon the throne,
Hosts His triumph gladly own!

Sweet it is to see Him there,
Centre of the glory fair,
Sweet our highest praise to bring,
Bow before the heavenly King!

Now within the Father's house,
There we know Him and rejoice;
Glad that He, e'en now, should share
All the Father's glory there.

Soon will He appear again,
Then His saints with Him shall reign.
Echo far the glorious words,
"King of kings" and "Lord of lords".

"My Glory"

JOHN 17 stands alone. It is the language of the Son as He addresses the Father on His own behalf and on that of the apostles and those who should believe on Him through their word. None but He, the Son of God, and both Shepherd and Advocate, could have breathed such a prayer. It was in no sense a pattern or model for the use of others, as was that which He gave to His disciples on an earlier day when He said to them, "After this manner pray ye."

There is no such injunction here, nor could be. It is the language of a faithful steward who recounts His work as done and well done. "I have finished", He says, "the work which Thou gavest me to do", speaking in anticipation of the moment, so near at hand, when He should loudly and triumphantly cry, "It is finished." On this ground He claims restoration to the glory which He had with the Father before the world was—a glory which He had never forfeited, a place which He had left in order to glorify God on earth in perfect manhood. He justly claims reinstatement in that place and in that glory which He had never dishonoured during His period of suffering here below. The defilement of earth had not affected Him. The water rises pure as ever to its level in the heavens.

Who but He could speak after this fashion? The prayer is therefore peculiarly His own. How worthy of our deepest meditation! What a privilege that we should be permitted to hear its sacred accents and to listen to the intercourse which passed between the Son and the Father at such a moment. Of the twenty-six verses of our chapter He spends but five on Himself; then follows eighteen which are occupied with the good of others, expressing as they do the most intense solicitude for their preservation from the evil of that world which He was about to leave, but wherein they were purposely left to fill His place in testimony and to exhibit the very unity of life and nature that existed between Himself and the Father. These verses, too, should be our constant and prayerful study. They will greatly enhance our appreciation of the Father—the holiness of His name, the sense of His preserving care, the blessedness of our relation to Him as children, and also the character of the world through which we are passing, its essential evil, its hatred of the Son, its ignorance of the Father, its absolute and hopeless alienation, even though grace may work in it, from all that is of the Father. How a clear sense of all this would, and should, draw together in holy separation from it those who love the Father and belong to the Son as given Him of that Father! Oh! for a deep realization of this new life, its meaning, the blessedness of the links that bind all the precious children of God together in relation with each other and the Father and the Son! What a conception! What a fact, and what a testimony! All will be gloriously accomplished ere long; and in the visible and indefectible display of this divine unity the world, so incredulous to-day, shall yet know that the

"MY GLORY"

Father sent the Son, and that, wondrous to say, He loved us (even us) as He loved the Son!

These eighteen verses—with all their wealth of interest, and their more than prayers for the preservation and unity of all His believing people—over, the blessed Lord, the Son loved of the Father—observe, "before the foundation of the world", and able, assuredly, on the ground of such a love so strong, so eternal—may well assert, in verse 24, His *will* as to those very people. Given of the Father, and purchased by His own precious blood, He may surely affirm His title to them. He may demand His personal gratification as to, first, their being with Him, where He is; and, second, that they should behold His glory—the glory given Him of the Father.

Just as a bridegroom would find pleasure in conducting his bride through their common home and in pointing out to her his varied possessions, so now the desire of the Lord is that those who had seen and shared His sorrows and who had, like Himself, been refused by the world should behold His glory. How great the difference! We have seen His cross, now we are to behold His crown!

That they may behold My glory! Not now the "moral glory" of chapter 1—that of an only-begotten Son with a Father, for this had been beheld, as we know; not now that of the Mount when He received from the Father honour and glory, for this, too, had been witnessed, but the glory given to Him as the result of His atoning death and suffering, a glory millennial indeed, but surely more extended than that, just as the effects of Calvary extend infinitely beyond the confines of time or the sceptre of the Messiah.

Nay, He seeks, and how rightly, His own gratification in the full and unreserved exhibition to "His own" of the glory which for ever shall be His God-given compensation for His anguish and agony, His obedience unto death, the death of the cross, here below. How richly deserved! "Father, I will", He says—it is no prayer, but the assertion of the same will, which in a few moments, was to be set aside for that of the Father and the necessity of the cross, when He prayed in the shades of the garden: "Not My will but Thine be done"—here He wills that those given Him of the Father may be with Him where He is, and why? "That they may behold My glory which Thou hast given Me." Yes, His gratification indeed, and as truly ours—mutual, eternal! It is His longed-for prospect and ours! And so soon, please God, to be realized! The *"will"* of verse 24 exceeds prayer, or petition, or demand. It is a claim. Demands had preceded; this, fully in accordance with the good pleasure of the Father, is a righteous title to those who are "His own" on the basis of everlasting love. The result is sure.

Verse 24 stands by itself. The two which follow are a beautiful summing up of the whole; the world is seen in its awful moral distance; the Father and Son are viewed in fullest intimacy, and the Father's name revealed perfectly to the highly favoured company which knows and possesses the love of the Father and the indwelling of the Son. Wondrous grace indeed. Oh! for hearts to worship and adore!

Praise

> "The race of God's anointed priests
> Shall never pass away.
> Before His glorious face they stand,
> And serve Him night and day."

A TRUER stanza was never penned. It was written some three hundred years ago; if true then it is true to-day.

The business of the priest is, first and foremost, to praise. He may have other sacred occupations, but praise is the chief.

"God inhabiteth the praises of Israel" (as we read in Psalm 22:3). Praise is His becoming environment. "Blessed are they that dwell in thy house, they will be still praising thee" (Psalm 84:4). Praise is their delightful and constant employment.

When a tribe was chosen to lead Israel across the desert, from sea to river, Judah was selected, and Judah means "praise". Alas that the harpers failed in their song!

Praise was the pæan of Jehoshaphat ere he fought his battle.

Stones would cry out if praise were restrained.

Prison walls only elicited praises when Christ's priests were, for His sake, placed in the stocks.

"Worthy is the Lamb" is the praise that reverberates throughout the wide vault of heaven. All is praise.

No, this race is immortal. It survives time with its thorns and hindrances, it shall continue for ever. It shall never pass away.

As surely as God has given His Spirit to a single soul—no matter when, or in what day or dispensation—that soul is hereby bound to sing His praise.

That Spirit is the pledged proof of blessing, and how can anyone be blessed without, subsequently, giving thanks and praise to the Blesser.

No doubt the fuller the light the deeper also the praise. The early notes of Ephesians 1 are a great advance on anything we find in the Old Testament; but, whether Old Testament or New, praise is the very life of the saint. Who then are God's "anointed priests"? Are they a special and distinctive class? Are they marked off from others by any external attire—anything that places them in a caste peculiar to themselves?

What is the anointing, the consecration, whereby their priesthood is assured? It is the reception of the Spirit of God. All who can truly cry "Abba Father", who can thus consciously address God, these are anointed; they have received His Spirit, and this is true of every child of His—every Christian to-day. They are a "royal priesthood" so that they should show forth the praises of Him who hath called them out of darkness into His marvellous light. The Christian community, the whole blood-bought family of God—the entire church of Christ, should be marked and distinguished by this grand special feature that, here and now, they show forth praise for the grace bestowed on them.

The apprehensions of all may differ, gifts may be diverse, but the one thing that declares the anointing is praise. That which God has done for His saints calls for their praise. Look at the Book of Psalms and see how it ends with a long, loud, lovely Hallelujah—a grand outburst of praise on the part of His redeemed and delivered people.

Quite true praise is not worship, but it is more than prayer and more too than thanksgiving.

We utter in prayer our wants, we give thanks for the gifts of God—His mercies and goodness; we praise Him for that which He has done, is doing and will do for our blessing—all this is in language articulate and audible, possibly, to the intelligence of men; but worship being the absorption of the soul in its glorious Object—the Father and the Son, may be beyond all possible expression. "The elders fell down and worshipped Him that liveth for ever and ever" (Revelation 5:14). What they said (if anything) we are not told.

Such worship! How little do we understand it! What a *terra incognita* it is to the majority of the children of God! But what a field for our increased apprehension, ere we find ourselves in the Father's House on high where our absorption in God fully revealed—Father, Son and Spirit—shall be eternal and complete.

Praise, on the other hand, as the true and simple acknowledgment of our being placed already in His "marvellous light" is the becoming language of every saint of His today.

But may it be cultivated diligently. May we charge our sluggish, selfish, grovelling hearts to live more in the bright, blessed region of praise to our God and Father as belonging to that "race of priests" which shall never pass away.

"Whoso offered praise glorifieth Me" (Psalm 50:23).

Bridal Affection and Brotherly Love

THERE never was a time when the affections of the church toward the Lord, as Bridegroom, should be more earnestly and diligently cultivated than the present moment.

His coming is drawing, we believe and hope, very near. With a deepening desire "the Spirit and the bride say, Come", as the day of union approaches. The bride bids Him welcome, as moved to do so by the animating Spirit to whom is known the mind of the Bridegroom. The desire is reciprocal; and if so, how fervently should the affections of the bride flow out to Him who not only loved her and gave Himself for her, but who shall presently come for her in person, and take her to be with Himself where He is for ever—"a glorious church, not having spot or wrinkle or any such thing, but holy and without blemish" (Ephesians 5:27).

Could anything be more seemly than such affection? Was it not departure from "first love" that originated the gradual fall of the church from days of pristine devotedness and zeal to the present state of Laodicean luke-warmness, worldliness, and widespread infidelity? And shall we not seek, at least individually, a return to that early love for our Lord Himself which at first made everything of Him and His sacred interests, while the world, with its snares and blandishments was a thing of naught? What but a deep appreciation of the love of Christ made the early church so separate, so holy, so devoted and the fire of those affections that burned up the attempts of the imitators, and endured the rage of opponents? The spring of love for the Lord was then supreme. He was everything to her—His bride—and she was, and, thank God, still is, everything to Him. He is the same, be the changing years what they may. "He loved them to the end."

And has there not been, for many years now, a gracious rekindling in the hearts of His saints of love for the Lord Himself? Has there not been a ministry of the Spirit which has had that, the chiefest of all ministry—the love of Christ—for its object, and a preparing of souls, not for an event, however blessed, but for the actual, personal coming of the Lord Himself?

This, I think, is undoubted. It can be traced through every cloud, and should be cherished in face of every opposition.

Let us remember that our Bible closes with the words: "Surely, I come quickly", and that the immediate and glad response is, "Even so, come, Lord Jesus." It is a beautiful close! It is the golden promise that was purposely given to cheer the heart of the bride through the, to our experience, long period of the Lord's absence; and not only to cheer her heart, but to test her allegiance and fidelity to Himself. We know, alas! the result, how the church has failed, but how that, spite of all, His love abides unaltered, while His promise is on the very eve of fulfilment. Hence, on these grounds alone our love for Him, our true, holy,

BRIDAL AFFECTION AND BROTHERLY LOVE

and bridal affections should centre increasingly on Himself.

What more comely, more suitable, more sanctifying?

Then, along with the development of such affections, there should be also that of brotherly love.

We need only turn to the First Epistle of John in order to learn the immense place which love to our fellow-Christians holds in the life of the true believer.

In chapter 2:10, we read that "he that loveth his brother abideth in the light". He is no longer in darkness, for "the light" is in his home, and love to his brother proves that he is there.

Further, in chapter 3:14: "We know that we have passed from death unto life, because we love the brethren." Thus we learn that love to our brethren is an absolutely essential mark of brotherhood in the divine family. It is the patent proof that we have passed out of death unto life. Not to love your fellow-Christian is, *de facto*, to hate him, as Cain hated and slew his brother, because, spite of his sacrifice, his works were evil and himself the same. He was not right with God, nor therefore with his brother. He stands before us as a fearful beacon. Then, again, in verse 23 of the same chapter we read: "And this is His commandment, that we should believe on the name of His Son, Jesus Christ, and love one another, as He gave us commandment." Mark the last word. It is His "commandment" that we should love one another. It is therefore our bounden and sacred duty that we should do so. None more binding nor obligatory; it is just as essential as is believing on the Son of God. Do we realize this duty? Do our renewed affections flow out not only to the Lord, our heavenly Bridegroom, but equally to each and all of God's beloved children? We are to love one another, as He has loved us (John 15:12). If only we did so, how soon would our strife and folly and divisions come to an end, or be happily reduced to a minimum.

But more (chapter 4:7-8), "Beloved, let us love one another, for love is of God, and everyone that loveth is born of God and knoweth God; he that loveth not, knoweth not God, for God is love." Two facts: first such an one is born of God—He possesses the divine nature; and, second he knows God. Not to love is not to know God (solemn thought indeed), for God is love. If the blessed God has been made known to the soul at all, He is known as love, and He has proved His love by the gift of His only begotten Son, that we might live through Him; and, yet again, that He might be the propitiation for our sins. How blessed! What pure and undeserved grace! How forceful the conclusion: "Beloved, if God so loved us, we ought also to love one another."

Hence, to love is the proof of being in the light; it is the consciousness of having passed from death unto life; it is the highest obligation of one Christian to another; and it is the reproduction and expression of the nature of that God who is love.

This is brotherly affection! How sacred! How necessary! How essential!

But, mark, in chapter 5:2 we find the salutary statement: "By this we know that we love the children of God when we love God and keep His commandments." Let this be noted: we only, and in truth, love His children when, first, we love God and keep His commandments. Our affections must be governed by the will of God, so that they may be of a nature divine, and not merely human; but all the deeper, purer, and more fervent on that account, as they flow forth to all His children.

May we cultivate all these precious affections in view of the near coming of the Lord, and also of the nature we possess as the children of God.

"For the Sake of the Name"

I QUOTE the above words from the Revised Version of the Third Epistle of John.

The Name! What name? "Because that for the sake of the name they went forth", writes the beloved Apostle.

In this brief, fervent letter three names are mentioned: that of Gaius, that of Diotrephes, and that of Demetrius, whilst certain others are spoken of as "strangers", but are unnamed.

Yet, with a significance which should command all attention, allusion is made to some one of whom "the name" is deemed sufficiently descriptive. It is clearly assumed that merely the word "name" calls for no elucidation. This is quite intelligible. If "the day" had a meaning of profound signification to some who thought of a moment which would bring a world-wide victory to their arms—"the day" which was whispered, and spoken of, as a secret, but which, having come, would exhibit the result of long years of expectant toil, how much more did "the name" pass as a watchword in the ranks of those early Christians who were the honoured subjects of the Apostles' ministry? That name stood pre-eminent with them; but shall it not do so to-day?

"FOR THE SAKE OF THE NAME"

As to the three men mentioned by name in the letter.

First, of Gaius we read that he enjoyed more prosperity of soul than of body; but spite of physical infirmities, he walked in truth and charity, and thus caused great joy to the heart of the Apostle, who had, indeed, no greater joy than to hear that his "children [in the faith, no doubt] walked in truth." But Gaius was a lover of hospitality; his charity was witnessed publicly. He maintained, in equipoise, the balance of truth and love—not love at the expense of truth, nor vice versa. He exemplified, in practice, the "better way" of 1 Corinthians 13. He was a fine specimen of an all-round Christian. No wonder that he gladdened the heart of the Apostle!

Second, Diotrephes comes before us, but in a deplorable contrast to Gaius. His sole object was self-exaltation; he loved to have pre-eminence (mark the word) in the church, refusing the Apostle himself and the brethren—the "strangers" referred to above, who "went forth for the sake of the name", forbidding those to receive them who would do so, and casting them out of the church. This is that Diotrephes! In him, cold, stern, hard officialism; rank, rigid ecclesiasticism, and a kind of papal tyranny combined with the zeal of a Jehu, outweighed the grace, patience, meekness, and lowliness that should characterize a servant of Christ. For such an one the Apostle had no regard. He would remember his deeds. He turns quickly away from thinking of Diotrephes; and, in his gentle style, he writes: "Beloved, imitate not that which is evil [let not the high-handed, merciless, inconsiderate ways of such an one be copied] but that which is good" (kind, profitable, beneficent); for, notice, "He that doeth good is of God [let these words sink into our consciences], but he that doeth evil hath not seen God." So much for Diotrephes!

Third, Demetrius. What of him? He carried "a good report of all, and of the truth itself". Happy Demetrius! Like the elders of Hebrews 11 his record was good. The truth had his name on its pages; the Apostle found pleasure in the very thought of him; he adorned the doctrines of Christ.

Each of these men had his history; but what of the mysterious name which exerted so great an influence over these "stranger" brethren who went forth expressly and solely for its exaltation, and under its exclusive authority, at all cost to themselves? What of its omnipotence, its charm, its all-sufficiency, its infinite magnetism over heart and mind and hand and foot—the name that captivated, that saved, that delivered, that constrained, that separated, that entranced, that controlled without a rival, that commanded, and that obtained obedience unqualified? What name was that?

It was not that of an apostle, nor of a church, nor of a school, nor of a mission. It favoured no party, nor clique, nor section, nor division. All such things were annihilated in the immensities of that name.

"He shall be called Wonderful, Counsellor, the mighty God, the everlasting Father [Father of eternity], Prince of peace" (Isaiah 9:6).

"God hath highly exalted Him and given Him a name which is above every name, that at the name of JESUS every knee should bow, and that every tongue should confess that Jesus Christ is Lord, to the glory of God the Father" (Philippians 2:9-11).

Now we understand why these devoted strangers "went forth". They had come under the spell of that name. It meant, first, their complete salvation—their purchase at a price incalculable—even His precious blood. They were slaves no more; they were Christ's free men and servants. He was their Lord and Master, their leader and commander, their treasurer and source of supply. From Him they had received and held their commission. They owned His absolute pre-eminence. These were some of the brethren whom Diotrephes would not receive! Then he should receive his own judgment. He may not be imitated. Happy it is to turn to a large-hearted, loving, and truthful Gaius; or to a record like that of the upright Demetrius, and seek to follow their faith while honestly and before God loathing the spirit of the wilful, place-seeking, domineering Diotrephes; or to tread humbly in the self-denying, devoted footsteps of the strangers and brethren who went forth, independently of man, simply and whole-heartedly "for the sake of the name".

It is just possible that this epistle was the last inspired writing. Anyhow, it is striking that the expression "THE NAME" should have such prominence. For these last days are, alas, witnesses of a vast Babel of party names; sects are distinguished by the names of men, of doctrines, of places, to our common shame, all of which would, if the supremacy of "THE NAME" were but owned, sink into their own miserable nothingness, as, thank God, they certainly shall, when, as the rising sun outshines all lesser luminaries, that Name which is above every name shall obliterate for ever the petty names and designations to which we attach so much puerile importance to-day. Oh! that the Spirit of God may magnify before the hearts of all the children of God the worth and glory and power and excellency of "THE NAME". It gives its outline to the Philadelphian.

The Last Psalm

"Praise ye the Lord."

1. Praise ye the Lord. Praise God in his sanctuary: praise him in the firmament of his power.
2. Praise him for his mighty acts: praise him according to his excellent greatness.
3. Praise him with the sound of the trumpet: praise him with the psaltery and harp.
4. Praise him with the timbrel and dance: praise him with stringed instruments and organs.
5. Praise him upon the loud cymbals: praise him upon the high sounding cymbals.
6. Let every thing that hath breath praise the Lord. Praise ye the Lord.

THE long voyage is over, and the harbour is reached; the roar of the storm gives place to the music of the haven. We have gained the end, the victory, the song.

Praise, and only praise, resounds on every hand. The voice of the enemy is silenced and his power is broken. The murmur of the wilderness is heard no more; its weary discords, its sobs, its pains, its sorrows, have given place to the glad "Hallelujah" of God's presence. Every heart is happy, and every mouth is filled with song. We are reminded of the parable of Luke 15, and the glad home where is received the once prodigal, its satisfaction and its music; only here the scope is wider. It is Israel replaced in its own land, in the joy of the kingdom, and in the presence of the King. The long night is over; the nation has received double for all its sins; its warfare is accomplished; iniquity is pardoned; it is the time of its "comfort". And what more befitting than such a song! What more comely than that instruments of music, the sweetest, the clearest, the loudest, should be employed to celebrate the praise of Jehovah?

There is now "no evil occurrent". The Lord is king, and His name is one, and His subjects are blessed. "Happy is the people that is in such a case; yea, happy is that people whose God is the Lord." They give heartfelt expression to their joy. In the six short verses of our beautiful closing psalm we have praise thirteen times. And what music! What harmony!

The heavenly sanctuary is invoked to sing praise to God (verse 1); not a voice in those glorious courts on high may be silent. They have their own exquisite song to sing in the glories of the Father's house, and in the knowledge of Father, Son, and Spirit fully revealed.

Then, again, "the firmament of His power" must reverberate with His praise. Not a being amid all these higher principalities but shall swell the chorus of His praise; while they who can sound trumpet, or psaltery, or harp, or timbrel, or pipe, or stringed instruments, or organs, or loud cymbals, or high sounding cymbals, shall also praise the Lord! Lovely orchestra, indeed, when each instrument of music emits in perfect and willing harmony the rightful praises of the Lord!

How glad the choristers, how sweet the song! But, in order to ensure the universality of the song, and to gather into its joy every intelligent being, the call is made: "Let every thing that hath breath praise the Lord." Breath, the breath of life, the faintest ability to articulate anything, let such, and all such, praise the Lord. Hallelujah!

What a conclusion! "Still praising" as ages roll. Happy service now and for ever on the part of the ransomed of the Lord.

Love's Retreat

HERE would I ever be,
   Close to His side,
Who in His love for me
   Willingly died.

Here would I ever lie,
   Down on His breast,
Proving so tenderly
   Heaven's own rest.

Here would I ever fall,
   Down at His feet,
Gladly to share with all
   Love's fond retreat.

Thus shall my spirit have
   Calmest repose,
When on life's stormy wave,
   Or amid foes.

Till my glad lip shall wake
   Heavenly song,
And the bright morn shall break
   Cloudless and long.

Then, Lord, my theme shall be
   Only Thy love,
And in Thy Father's house,
   Heaven above,

I shall Thy beauty trace,
   Vision sublime,
There see Thy wealth of grace,
   Glory divine.

www.ingramcontent.com/pod-product-compliance
Lightning Source LLC
Chambersburg PA
CBHW060341050426
42449CB00011B/2807